PENNY THE RAILWAY PUP

BOOK 4 IN THE FAMILY OF RESCUE DOGS
SERIES

BRIAN L PORTER

INTRODUCTION

Welcome to the fourth book in my series about the lives of the rescued dogs that share our lives and our home. Those of you who've read the previous books in the series will be familiar with the names of most of the dogs that currently form our little 'pack' of rescues, but in Penny's case, I felt this short introduction would be useful. Why? Well, Penny has been with us longer than all our dogs with the exception of Dylan, whose story will be coming in due course. That being the case, regular readers might find it strange to read the names of some of the dogs that appear in this book, as the make-up of our pack has changed over the years, with some of the dogs having passed over the Rainbow Bridge in the intervening years. As this is Penny's story, I have deliberately avoided including the upsetting details of those wonderful furry friends who are no longer with us.

So, please go ahead and enjoy the story of Penny, The Railway Pup. Why railway pup, I hear one or two of you asking? To understand the title, you need to read the book!

Note to my U.S. readers:
A short glossary

Although I didn't feel it necessary to include a glossary with this book, I do feel I should point out, for the benefit of my American readers, that here in the U.K. we use the word *'lead'* instead of the American 'leash'.

Estate car – station wagon.

I should also mention the phrase *'sea front'* used in chapter 7, relating to our visit to Scarborough. This refers to what I believe my American friends and readers would refer to as the 'boardwalk,' the area which runs along the length of the beach, and which features various shops, amusement arcades, cafes etc.

So, there you go, the world's shortest glossary!

Brian and Penny today

1

BEFORE PENNY

IT WAS A NORMAL AUTUMN AFTERNOON, and I arrived at the vet with our cairn terrier, Charlie, sadly no longer with us, for his annual booster vaccination. The sun was shining, and the vet's waiting room was almost deserted as Charlie and I entered and announced our arrival to the receptionist. Let me explain that because Juliet and I owned a number of rescued dogs - I think we had eight or nine at the time this occurred - we knew all the staff at the surgery and were on first name terms with them. On this particular day, we were booked in by Lisa, who smiled warmly and asked if she could have a word with me before I left that afternoon. Intrigued, I agreed to see her on our way out, wondering what she might want to tell me.

Charlie was soon attended to and we exited the treatment room and made our way to the reception desk to pay for his injection and, of course, to find out what Lisa had to say to me. There were no other patients waiting as I paid Charlie's bill. Lisa passed me my receipt for the fee and smiled at me again. *What was she smiling at?* I wondered.

"Right then, Lisa, what have you got to tell me?" I asked.

Still smiling, Lisa replied, "I don't suppose you know anyone who might be prepared to give a home to a little terrier do you?"

I quickly realised why Lisa had had that smile plastered on her face from the moment I'd walked in through the surgery doors. Like everyone at the practice, she was well aware that Juliet and I had a number of rescued dogs at home and obviously felt we would be amenable to taking in another one.

"I don't know, Lisa," I responded. "I can't really say much without knowing anything about the dog, and of course, Juliet would have a say in any new adoptions, too. What can you tell me about the dog?"

Lisa then surprised me by explaining that the dog was currently in her care, but that she was seeking a permanent home for the terrier.

"I have her at home," she went on, "but I have three of my own dogs in the house and can't really fit another one in. She's living outside in a pen, alongside my breeding dogs at present."

Lisa explained that she had a purpose-built area in her back yard where she bred Dogue de Bordeauxs. The terrier was taking up one of the pens at present but would be much better living in a home with a nice family.

"I've been thinking of asking you for a while but this is the first chance I've had," she said. My house itself isn't very big, so I really can't keep her inside, or we'd be overcrowded."

"What kind of dog is she?" was my next question.

"She's a Jack Russell cross."

"And how come she's ended up with you, and what's her name? I'm going to have to talk about this with Juliet, so I'm not making any promises."

"I understand that, but I'm sure if you came and had a look at her, you'd be happy with her. She doesn't really have a name, but I call her Pancake because she was brought to me on Pancake Day."

For non-UK readers, I should explain that 'Pancake Day' is actually Shrove Tuesday, once of religious significance, though rarely celebrated as such in the UK nowadays. It is the Tuesday before Ash Wednesday, when pancakes are traditionally served.

"Okay, so how did you come to get her?"

"It's a long story," said Lisa, who went on to explain where she lived, so I'd have a better idea of what she was about to tell me. "Until recently there was a gypsy encampment on the waste ground near the railway station. One tea-time, there was a knock at my door and two little girls were standing there, maybe eight to ten years old, with the older of the two holding a puppy in her arms. You could tell they were sisters just by looking at them. They told me they'd been out playing and saw that the gypsies had gone so they went to take a look in the field near the station where they'd camped, in case they'd left anything behind. From the scruffy state of their clothes, their white socks covered in mud and muck, and their dirty faces, I could tell they'd had a really good time exploring the old gypsy site."

"And they found the puppy?"

"Not at first. They told me they had looked all-round the site where the gypsies had parked their trucks and caravans etc. but had found nothing interesting, at least nothing that would attract a couple of young junior school girls. Then, they walked towards the railway station, and on the other side of the fence, they saw something moving a few yards along the tracks. They soon realised that what they were seeing was a little dog. They called out to the puppy but, although it was moving, it didn't make any attempt to go to them. They followed the fence and when they got closer, they realised that the puppy had a rope round its neck and that the rope was caught up on the track. The sisters realised that the poor little thing was stuck and could do nothing to free itself. They were also intelligent enough to realise that, if a train came along, the poor little puppy would probably be hit and killed by the engine. Although they knew it was a dangerous thing to do, as well as being against the law to trespass on the tracks, the two girls climbed over the fence and ran to the puppy, who was excited to see them. They told me it took them a couple of minutes to free the puppy from the track, and the elder girl picked her up and cuddled and reassured her. They couldn't tell if the little dog had run away from the gypsy camp and got trapped accidentally, or if the gypsies had abandoned her, and left her tied to the railway track."

"That's horrific," I interrupted. "But, how did they know to take her to your house?"

"A lot of the local kids know me, and come to see my horses quite often. They know I work for a vet and that I breed dogs. They call me, 'the vet lady.' So, the girls struggled between them to carry her to my house and knocked on my door."

This was the first I'd heard of Lisa owning horses, so I presumed she must have quite a large home. She soon corrected me when she explained her home was an old terraced house that had been modernised and that she rented the adjoining field, where she kept her two horses. Like many of the older houses in the area where she lived, it had a large rear 'garden' which she'd converted into breeding kennels, but the interior of the house was relatively small.

Before going on with her story, she paused to book in a newly arrived patient and its owner and then she continued.

"So, what could I do?" she asked. "The girls had rescued an abandoned puppy and they explained they'd first taken the little dog home but their Mum wouldn't let them keep it, so they'd thought of me. I didn't have much choice, so I agreed to take the pup in and see if I could find it a good home."

"And you thought of us?"

"No, not right away. I've had her for about nine months. I just never got around to seriously looking to re-home her but recently, I thought it would be better for her if she could live in a nice home with a family, instead of living in a pen and not having a proper home-life. She gets lots of exercise and play-time in the field of course, but it's not the same is it?"

I agreed with what she said and agreed to speak to Juliet when I got home. I left the surgery with her address and phone number on a piece of paper and of course, wasted no time informing Juliet about the little dog when I returned home with Charlie.

Juliet, whose thoughts on dog rescue entirely match my own (or we could never do what we do), agreed that we should at least take a look at the little dog in Lisa's care, so I picked up the phone and called Lisa, who was still at work. We arranged to go over and see the dog the following day, which happened to be her day off. We told our two girls who were excited at the prospect of having a new dog to add to our family and they went to bed that night with their minds already made up. Juliet and I were at least a little more pragmatic, though I think that deep down both of us felt we couldn't leave the young dog living in a pen any longer than necessary. Lisa had turned to us for help and we both knew that, miracles aside, we would give the pup a home if we liked what we saw and felt she could fit in with our little pack of rescued dogs.

2

'PANCAKE'

THE FOLLOWING DAY, the girls were home from school in record time. Both of them attended the local junior school and they came running out of the gate to be met by Juliet. They were around six and seven years old at the time. They virtually ran all the way home, with Juliet being carried along in their wake, such was their excitement at going to see the dog later that day. Both of them were so excited they hardly touched their tea when Juliet put it down on the table. They kept asking how long it was until we went to see the dog. They wanted us to take one or two of our dogs with us to meet the pup, but Juliet and I explained that it wouldn't be a good idea, as Lisa had dogs of her own, and horses too, and we didn't want to upset the horses or scare the little pup by suddenly appearing with one or two dogs it had never met before. They understood what we were telling them, and became excited at the prospect of seeing Lisa's horses as well as the little dog.

Soon enough, the time came for us to leave for our visit to see the dog. We were soon loaded into the car and driving the five or six miles to where Lisa lived. The village was one that used to be what we call a 'pit village', in close proximity to a coal mine that had sadly closed some years previously and had left behind a shattered community, with most of the area giving off a downtrodden and hopeless atmosphere. In such a village, most of the working population worked at the pit, either above or underground, and as a result of its closure, unemployment was at record levels within the once-proud mining community. Many of the streets comprised houses in dire need of repair and most of the shops on the main street were either closed and boarded up, or looked close to ending up that way. A once thriving community, so dependent on what was once named *King Coal* now appeared to be dying on its feet.

Lisa's home was on the outskirts of the village, close to open fields. The street where she lived showed signs of regeneration, with the houses having been bought by private buyers like Lisa. They were being repaired and modernised, a sure sign of hope for the future of the village, which, I'm pleased to say, has slowly rebuilt itself and its sense of civic pride in the intervening years.

Lisa welcomed us at the front door and led us through the house, exiting through the back door into a long garden and a yard that held her breeding kennels. She showed us the field just a little way from the gate at the end of her garden, and her two horses came slowly ambling up to the fence to greet her. She took two carrots from her pocket, giving the girls one each, to feed to the horses, which both animals clearly enjoyed. The girls loved seeing and feeding the horses, and Lisa allowed them to stroke their faces, but by then they were both impatient to see the little dog.

After the horses had finished their carrots, Lisa asked us to wait where we were and she'd bring the dog out to see us. A couple of minutes passed, with the girls stroking the horses, both of whom were extremely friendly, bending their heads over the fence so they could stroke their faces. Suddenly we saw a little black and white dog appear from the kennels, and it came running straight towards us.

She was a lovely little thing, mostly white, with black ears and eye patches, and a black patch where her body joined her tail. She had a long tail, that wagged constantly as she ran happily in our direction. When she reached us, she stopped and began saying hello in her own way, jumping up and down, wagging her tail, and making a big fuss of us all in turn.

Lisa arrived a few seconds afterwards with a big smile on her face.

"I see you're getting acquainted," she said.

"You could say that," I replied. "She's definitely a friendly little thing, isn't she?"

"She loves everybody," said Lisa, who walked a few yards to where a deflated football lay on the ground. Picking it up, she threw the ball and the little dog immediately chased after it, scooping it up in her mouth. Despite its size, the fact it held no air enabled her to hold on to it and she happily ran along, keeping it above the ground, occasionally stopping to toss it around, still in her mouth, shaking it in a typical terrier-like motion as though she was tossing a rat about.

"Playful, too I commented."

"How does she get along with other dogs?" Juliet asked.

"Perfectly," Lisa replied. "Never had a problem in that respect."

Juliet and I spent the following fifteen minutes playing with the dog, who showed us lots of love and affection, with licks, tail-wags and even rolling over on to her back for a tummy rub, or two. It quickly became clear she was a happy, loving little thing and we soon agreed we'd like to offer her the home she deserved.

"Do you want anything for her?" I asked Lisa.

"Oh no," she replied. "I just want her to have a good home.

"When can we take her?"

"Right now, if you want."

Of course, the girls immediately chorused, "Oh please, can we take her home with us?" and the decision was made.

Lisa helped us to the car and gave 'Pancake' a last stroke and cuddle before we closed the tailgate and prepared to drive home. "Be good," she said, and the little terrier wagged her tail furiously.

"We'll probably be changing her name," I told Lisa, not wanting to upset her.

"That's okay," she said. "She was never really my dog anyway. I had to call her something and that was appropriate as Pancake Day was the day she arrived here. You call her what you want."

The drive home only took us a few minutes and during that time, we'd decided that, as she'd spent most of her life in a pen, we'd called her Penny. She was like a new puppy when we first entered our house with her. There was something about Penny, that seemed to exude peacefulness, to the extent that, unusually, our other dogs barely seemed to notice we'd brought another dog into the house.

That may seem strange but it's true. It took some of them a few minutes to notice her and even then, they just appeared to wander up to her, have a sniff at her, one or two touched noses with her, and that was it. We'd never had such an easy introduction of a new dog into the home. Penny took to the house like a duck to water, quickly exploring her new surroundings, her tail wagging with happiness all the time.

The only worry we had was that she may not be house trained, having spent so long living in a pen, but from the very first day, Penny never did a single pee, or made any mess in the house. Talk about a perfect dog!

It was evening already and Penny happily joined our other dogs at feeding time, hungrily eating up every morsel of food in her bowl. She joined me and couple of our other dogs, Charlie and Molly the Westie for a short walk, walking perfectly on her new lead, just to get her acclimatised to her new surroundings. She was lucky that we always kept a couple of spare leads in the house and the one we gave her was a red one with pink hearts on it, perfect for a little girl dog.

We always kept a spare dog bed in the shed and Juliet had prepared it for her, with a couple of nice, warm fluffy blankets. At bedtime, Penny joined the other dogs as they went out into the garden before snuggling down comfortably in her new, cosy bed, and she was asleep in no time.

Pancake had become Penny and she now had a home of her own at last.

New home, new 'hair-do'

3

EARLY DAYS

PENNY'S first few days in our home were a sheer delight as she settled in to our family as if she'd been with us forever. The other dogs had accepted her without any fuss whatsoever and she responded to all the love and affection she was given by giving us the same in return.

On her very first morning with us, I decided to take her with me when I took four of our dogs to run and play on the nearby playing field. For some reason, both Juliet and I had decided the risks of Penny running away were minimal if I let her off-lead to play with the other dogs, so, after I let her watch the other dogs running and playing for a couple of minutes, I unclipped her lead and let her run free.

I admit, I breathed a big sigh of relief, when our faith in Penny had proved itself as she ran straight for the other dogs and joined in with their doggy playtime. I threw a few tennis balls for them and Penny loved the new game as they brought the balls back to me to be thrown again, and again, and again!

By the end of Penny's first 'walk' with me, I was worn out from ball-throwing. The next day I went out and purchased one of those plastic ball launchers. At least it would save some of the strain on my arm and shoulder. Later that day she enjoyed her first walk with Juliet, who introduced her to the members of what we jokingly called the 'dog club.' This was simply a daily gathering of dog owning friends, who would meet on the larger playing field, not far from our home, where everyone could safely let their dogs run free and play together. We wondered how Penny would get along with this group of strangers, but as Juliet later reported to me, she had a great time playing with the other dogs, and all the humans made a great fuss of her, which she adored. She spent almost the entire time on the field with her tail seemingly set to 'permanent wag'. I had to laugh though, as Juliet said to me,

"It was so funny, I couldn't help laughing when Linda and a couple of the others said it was nice of us to have adopted an older dog. I told them she was less than eighteen months old and they could hardly believe it."

We then realised why people might think she was a senior dog. Penny's markings are such that her black ears and eye patches are interspersed with quite a lot of white hairs, and at first glance, a person might think she was indeed an older dog whose fur was turning grey. All these years later, Penny looks exactly as she did when we first adopted her, so I suppose, at last, our friends are now correct in their assumptions that she's an old dog. After all the years she's been with us, she finally is one!

When not running around playing ball, Penny showed herself to be the (almost) perfect dog to take on a lead walk, trotting perfectly by my side, or with Juliet. In time, we could trust her to walk by our side without a lead, as long as we weren't near any roads or traffic of any kind. We would never take that chance with any of our dogs, no matter how well-trained they are, and that decision was vindicated one day when, as I was walking with her along a street near our home, and a car drove passed us, quite close to the kerb, Penny suddenly leaped at the car, and it was lucky for her that I was holding on to her lead, otherwise she could have been hurt if she'd collided with a moving vehicle. We hoped this might be an isolated incident but over the next few weeks we realised that Penny had some kind of mental aversion to the sound of vehicles 'whooshing' past her while she was out walking. This seemed to be even worse if it was, or had been, raining as the sound of the tyres on the wet road surface really appeared to annoy her. As well as trying to jump at the car, she'd start barking at it, very loudly. Believe it or not, it took a lot of training and about five years to finally cure Penny of this unusual habit, though we were never really able to ascertain exactly what triggered this rather strange behaviour. Did our attempts to train it out of her work, or did she simply 'grow out' of the habit? We'll never know!

What we do know is that Penny settled in to our home in no time at all and everyone who met our latest rescue girl fell in love with her almost immediately. With such a happy attitude to life and a peaceful and passive demeanour it would have been hard not to.

Juliet is a qualified groomer and soon after Penny's arrival, she decided to give her a good tidy up, so one Saturday, she lifted her onto the grooming table and set to work. A while later she stood back to admire her handiwork and called me to come and take a look. Penny looked terrific. Her fur had, until then, been quite long and shaggy. Now, she almost looked like a different dog. Not only did she look sleek and smooth, but it was possible to see, that underneath her long fur, her skin was covered in black spots, rather like those of a Dalmation. She also looked much slimmer. One or two people had commented on her, believing her to be overweight, but under all that fur, she was as trim as any of our other dogs. Nowadays, Juliet lets her fur grow through the winter months to help her keep warm in the cold weather, then trims her back to her 'summer coat' when the warmer spring weather arrives. People still make comments about her weight, which we've learned to ignore over the years. Whenever she visits the vet for her annual vaccination booster or for anything else, we have her weighed and her weight has always remained pretty much the same over the years, so, overweight? Definitely not!

After we'd had her for a while it suddenly dawned on me that I hadn't asked Lisa if Penny had been spayed, so I made a quick phone call to her and she assured me she'd had Penny 'done' some time ago. It wouldn't have been a good idea to risk any accidental coupling, what with her stud dogs around! She also asked me to call in at the surgery when she was next on duty, and she'd give me Penny's vaccination card and microchip certificate so we could change the details to our name and address. In the excitement of first getting Penny, those little details had been understandably forgotten. As she was at work the next day, I called in with Penny in-tow, sorted out the paperwork and Lisa was pleased to see how well she was doing. Of course, Penny made a big fuss of her, and all the other staff, who naturally fell for her charms and it took me about twenty minutes to make our exit from the vet's surgery, as everyone wanted to make a big fuss of her. Lisa was also impressed with Penny's new 'hair do.'

* * *

TIME SEEMED to fly past as Penny settled in and soon became a happy and well-loved member of our little pack of rescues. Apart from the jumping at cars habit she seemed to have no vices. She was so easy going, and so placid. Everyone who met her seemed to fall in love with the sweet-natured little terrier. We spent some time trying to determine what her heritage might be, for it was obvious she wasn't a full Jack Russell. With her short stubby legs, which were shaped like those of an old-fashioned 'Queen Anne' table, her extra-long tail, and her gentle temperament, she was, in many ways, very un-terrier-like.

In the end, we could only conclude, bearing in mind she was raised in a gypsy encampment, that our beautiful little Penny was simply a good old-fashioned mongrel. Not for her, any of today's fancy names that some people like to give to various cross-breeds. Our Penny is a beautiful, fluffy little star, no matter what breed she is.

Penny with her ball

4

ATTACKED!

PENNY LOVED TO PLAY. Of that there was no doubt at all.
Tennis balls, deflated footballs (soccer variety), discarded
plastic bottles, any kind of toy she could chase and bring back,
you name it, she'd play with it. She was without doubt a happy
dog, and always seemed to have a spring in her step as she
trotted along beside me on her walks.

Anyone who has read *Cassie's Tale* will already know that
our dogs had a great doggie friend, Cindy, a little Yorkshire
Terrier who, with her owner, Maureen, would usually join us
on the nearby playing field, at least once, and often twice a day.
Cindy had been attacked by a large dog when she was a mere
puppy and had spent most of her life in fear of other dogs.
Maureen had quite sensibly refrained from letting her off her
lead during their walks ever since, until she'd met me and our
dogs. Cindy and Cassie soon became the best of friends and
before long, Maureen felt confident and brave enough to try
letting Cindy off her lead, at least while she was in the
company of me and my dogs. Over a period of time, Cindy and
Cassie even began to devise their own 'doggie games' including

the most amusing 'nose tennis,' whereby the two of them would literally 'bat' a tennis ball back and forth between them, propelled, as the name suggests, by the tips of their noses.

Penny soon became a part of this little group and loved running around on the field, usually with a tennis ball of her own, which I'd throw or kick for her to chase and bring back, a game she needed no training to play. Talking of training brings to mind my amusing memories of taking Penny to dog training classes.

A good friend of mine, also called Brian, happened to be one of the North of England's finest canine behaviourists, and he had started a series of dog training classes not too far from our home. Every Saturday lunchtime, I would be joined, usually by both Rebecca and Victoria, and we'd load four or sometimes five of the dogs into the rear of the car, (back then we had a large Mondeo estate car) and drive the few miles to participate in Brian's classes. Among other things, one of the activities he taught was dog agility, and most of our dogs absolutely loved it.

Penny, however, was one of the rare exceptions. Whether it was her short little legs, or just her over-playful nature, Penny just couldn't come to terms with the agility course. Like all newcomers to agility, we began by slowly walking her round the course on her lead, but when it came to any form of climbing or jumping, Penny much preferred going around the obstacles, rather than going over them. It was actually quite funny to see, as her playful nature came to the fore, and when we allowed her to try going off-lead she made everyone laugh as she negotiated the course with a series of high-speed swerves and skips. She did it with such a look on her face and with her tail wagging and swaying behind her, that it was impossible to get angry at her failure to make a serious attempt to learn this new skill. After three or four weeks of trying, we gave up the agility training and tried her with the game of Flyball. Bad mistake! Anything involving a tennis ball was pure joy for Penny, but the trouble was, when on the Flyball course, she simply refused to give up the ball, preferring instead to veer off course and run around with the ball in her mouth, before deciding to bring it to me, expecting me to throw it for her to play 'fetch' with. Of course, the other owners found it hilarious, as I did too, and even Brian the trainer knew enough to acknowledge when he was beaten. From that day, as far as Penny was concerned, we concentrated on the basics of dog training, stay, come here, you get the idea? It seemed that no matter where we went and no matter what we did with her, Penny was a source of fun and entertainment for everyone she came into contact with.

When we thought of the start in life she'd had, Juliet and I had to admit that Penny had developed so well. She was well behaved, (apart from the car problem, which she gradually grew out of), obedient, never, never made a mess or did a pee in the home, and certainly never caused any problems with other dogs, either our own or anyone else's.

Unfortunately, one day, completely out of the blue, Penny became the victim of a completely unprovoked attack by another, much larger dog which appeared to have strayed onto the playing field. One minute she was happily running around, playing with her tennis ball and the next, she was literally screaming in agony as the unknown dog seemed to appear from nowhere at high speed and literally launched itself at poor Penny.

The dog was a medium to large crossbreed and though I fully expected its owner to come running after it within a few seconds, nobody appeared. Everything was happening so fast, but I did manage to see that the dog had no collar and therefore no identity tag. As poor Penny squealed, and I tried my best to 'shoo' the dog away, without getting bitten myself, who should intervene but my pack leader, Tilly. The little cross breed terrier ran across from the other side of the playing field, where she'd been playing with Charlie and Molly, and literally launched herself on to the back of the attacker. Not liking the way the odds had turned against it, the attacker suddenly broke off its assault on Penny, seemed to twist in min-air and turned its attention to Tilly, biting at her and taking a chunk out of her side. Undeterred, Tilly went back at the dog, who quickly decided it didn't like the way things were going, and suddenly turned tail and ran, heading back in the direction it had come from.

Tilly the heroine

With everything calm once more, I was able to assess the damage to my dogs. As Charlie and Molly came across to join us, I could see that Penny was in a bit of a mess. There seemed to be blood everywhere, mostly around her rear end, and Tilly was bleeding from the bite sustained to her side. I used my mobile phone to call home and Juliet was with us within five minutes. We got our dogs home and quickly tried to clean up some of the blood from Penny's wounds to see just how bad her injuries were. It really was bad and the bleeding just wouldn't stop. Tilly's wound was not as bad as it first appeared. It was fairly superficial, but nasty nonetheless.

I phoned our vet who advised me to bring both dogs in, right away, and we quickly loaded the dogs into the car, with a large blanket wrapped round Penny to try and stem the bleeding. We were seen immediately on arrival at the surgery, where the vet decided that Penny's injuries were quite serious. She would need multiple stitches and antibiotics to prevent infection from her bite wounds. This meant she'd require a general anaesthetic and I'd have to leave her at the surgery, where they would operate immediately. Tilly's wound was, as expected, superficial and didn't need stitches, but they did take her through to the treatment area while I waited. They cleaned her wound, gave her antibiotic and painkilling injections to protect against infection and she was soon back with me, together with a course of antibiotics to take at home, as well as painkillers for five days.

Penny wasn't so lucky. After a full examination the vet informed me that the attack had not just resulted in bites, but that a large flap of skin was hanging off. He said they would do their best to re-attach it, and the operation would take a little longer than first thought. It was arranged that I would return near closing time to collect her and, for the time being, Tilly and I returned home without our little Penny.

It was almost lunchtime by the time I arrived home and was able to reassure a very worried Juliet that Penny would be okay after the operation to repair the damage to her rear. Neither of us felt like eating much and we spent the rest of the day worrying about Penny. We still had the other dogs to walk of course, apart from Tilly, who had been ordered to rest for at least 24 hours by the vet. Tilly was truly our heroine that day. Without her timely intervention, the outcome could have been far worse for Penny. Though we spent an anxious afternoon as we waited for the phone call that would tell us how the operation had gone, we also made sure Tilly received lots of fuss and treats as a reward for her bravery, even though she couldn't understand why she wasn't allowed to accompany me on our usual afternoon walk.

Later that afternoon, the vet phoned. Penny had come thorough the operation okay, and, as previously arranged, I could collect her later that day. She was obviously still sleepy from the anaesthetic, but would be fully conscious very soon. He also told me he would show me what they'd had to do when I arrived at the surgery; her rear-end had been in a real mess, as they'd discovered, once she was on the operating table.

"That doesn't sound too good," I said, with obvious worry in my voice.

"Don't worry, he replied. "It's just that it will be easier to show you rather than explain over the phone. Penny will be just fine."

"Okay," I said, breathing a sigh of relief."

"I'll see you in a couple of hours," he went on, "and as I said, please don't worry."

Juliet and I spent the rest of the afternoon doing our usual dog walks, and after feeding them at their usual time, I found myself becoming restless as the time seemed to drag while I waited for the close of surgery so I could go and bring our little girl home. The wait was excruciating so, in the hope I could maybe collect her a little earlier than we'd arranged, I phoned the surgery to see if it would be possible.

21

After I'd hung on for a couple of minutes, the receptionist, who'd answered the phone and then gone to speak to the vet, returned to the phone and informed me that it would be okay if I wanted to go a bit earlier, in half an hour, in fact. That was fine by me and very soon, I was in the car once more, heading for the vet's surgery.

When I arrived, the receptionist greeted me with a smile. At that moment, one of the veterinary nurses came out from the treatment area and also smiled when she saw me.

"Penny's been just great," she said. "What a little star she is, a perfect patient. I've been giving her lots of cuddles since she came round, bless her. She's a really brave little girl. She hasn't whinged or cried at all since she's been fully awake. I'll let the vet know you're here and we won't keep you waiting long."

I thanked her and sat on one of the waiting room chairs. Within a couple of minutes, she popped her head around the door and called me in to the consulting room. The vet, Bernard, was there, with Penny already up on the table so he could show me what they'd done to repair her wounds. Poor Penny did look a mess, despite all they'd done to help her. Her rear-end just appeared to be a mass of never-ending stitches, resembling a patchwork quilt, and of course, they'd had to shave a lot of her fur off so they could work on the damaged flesh underneath.

"Penny's been very lucky," he said. "I'm glad you got her to us so quickly. She'd lost a lot of blood and the dog that attacked her really did make a mess of her, as you can see. Are you sure you couldn't identify the culprit?"

"No," I explained, as I gently stroked Penny's head. "It had no I.D. tag or collar and I'd never seen it before so I've no idea who the owner is."

"Shame," Bernard replied. "I just hope it doesn't do this to any more dogs."

"Me too. So, what is it you need to explain to me?" I said, referring back to what he'd told me over the phone.

Over the next few minutes, he pointed out the work they'd done on Penny's wounds and then came to the point he'd been waiting to tell me.

"The other dog took quite a chunk of skin from here." He pointed to the area around her bottom. "To prevent the danger of necrosis setting in, I had to remove quite a bit of the flap of skin and pull the skin together, and then stitch her up. So, it will probably feel a bit tight, and certainly very tender for Penny in that area for a couple of weeks until the skin heals and begins to knit itself together again. I'm giving you some strong painkillers for her. She's already had a painkilling injection and an antibiotic injection so you don't need to start the tablets until tomorrow." The nurse passed me two bottles of tablets.

"These are her painkillers," she said as she handed me the first bottle, "and these are antibiotics to prevent infection," as she gave me the second bottle.

The vet also wanted to give me a 'buster collar,' one of those horrible cone-shaped plastic collars that help prevent the dog from getting at and licking its stitches etc. I quickly explained I wouldn't need it. When you have a pack of dogs such as we have, taking a dog into the house wearing one of those tends to turn the dog into a 'target' for the other dogs who become incredibly inquisitive and simply won't leave the dog wearing it, alone. As a result, there is a possibility, not only that the collar itself can be damaged, but the other dogs can end up causing further damage to the operation area. We have become accustomed, over the years, to ensuring our dogs don't interfere with any of our dogs that have undergone surgery, and have never encountered a problem. The vet was happy enough to bow to our experience and leave Penny's convalescence in our hands.

"Keep her as still and as quiet as possible when you get her home," the vet instructed me. "Try and keep your other dogs from sniffing at her wounds. I wouldn't want one of them to accidentally disturb the stitches, so try and keep her isolated as much as you can."

I assured him that wouldn't be a problem. Both the vet and the nurse accompanied me out of the room and the vet informed the receptionist that he wanted me to get Penny home as soon as possible. He said that I could call and fill in the necessary forms for the pet insurance claim when I brought Penny back in three days, as he wanted to give her a post-operative check a little sooner than usual, due to the nature of the injuries. The receptionist quickly booked Penny in for her post-op check at a convenient time for me, and both the vet and the nurse came to the car with me, the vet gently carrying Penny for me. When I opened the tailgate, he gently placed Penny on the big dog cushion we always keep in the car for the dogs. Juliet had replaced the earlier, by now blood-stained blanket with a new, clean one, which the nurse tenderly placed over Penny, to ensure she stayed warm on the journey home. Penny was already half-asleep, the effects of the anaesthetic still lingering in her system.

I thanked them both profusely and before setting off for home, I called Juliet from my mobile phone and quickly explained what the vet had told me. She said she'd move Penny's bed into the hallway, where she could be isolated from the other dogs by the baby gate we use to prevent them from going upstairs during the day. I drove home slowly and very carefully, so as not to jostle Penny around too much on the journey and ten minutes later we pulled up outside our house.

Juliet was waiting at the front door and she came out to the car to help me to take Penny into the house. I opened the tailgate and we looked in the back to find little Penny had fallen asleep on the short journey home. My careful driving and the gentle movement of the car, combined with the effects of the anaesthetic had lulled her into a nice, deep sleep. Juliet carefully picked her up, and Penny just sort of opened her eyes, sleepily, and then closed them again. As we entered the house, there was her bed, ready and waiting for her in the hall, and Juliet gently laid her in it, with Penny opening her eyes again for a few seconds, before once again falling asleep.

Most of our other dogs, filled with inquisitiveness, appeared from the kitchen or the lounge, wanting to see what was going on. They couldn't actually get close to Penny due to the baby gate doing its job, but they seemed to take it in turns to stand at the gate, looking at Penny, their noses invariably twitching as they viewed their little friend in her bed, looking very poorly and sorry for herself. Of course, they were intelligent dogs, and they could smell VET! After checking her out, they all seemed to realise Penny wasn't well, and they all left her in peace for the rest of the evening.

Leaving Penny to rest and sleep, Juliet and I moved to the lounge, where the girls were waiting. Juliet had previously told them to wait there while we brought Penny into the house, but now we allowed them to go and see her with strict instructions to not disturb her, as she needed rest to help her to get better.

She certainly had some way to go, but at least, after the horrors of the morning, little Penny was safely back home and ready to begin her journey on the road to recovery.

Relaxing, on the road to recovery

5

OH NO. NOT AGAIN!

THE FOLLOWING DAY, after Penny had managed a good night's sleep in her own bed, we had a chance to take a good look at the extent of her wounds and the results of her operation. We were amazed at the amount of stitches the vet had been forced to use to close up her wounds. They were impossible to count. In the end, Juliet and I estimated there were something in the region of sixty to seventy altogether. Most of them were concentrated in the area where the flap of skin had been hanging off. We could now understand what the vet had explained to me, when he told me he had needed to literally pull the two ends of the skin together after thoroughly cleaning out the wound, before commencing to stitch everything together. He'd also instructed me to watch the wound carefully, as there was a danger of necrosis taking hold of the skin flap which would result in the skin actually dying. We had to make sure the area remained clean and we needed to bathe the area twice a day with a saline solution.

Poor Penny must have been in a lot of pain, but she was such a good dog and tried to carry on as normal, even though it would be a while before things were 'normal' again for her. When we were getting ready to take the other dogs for their walks, her tail would wag and she'd do her best to stand up and tell us it was her turn to go out as well. Unfortunately for Penny, it would be some weeks before she would be well enough to go out for even the shortest of walks.

In the meantime, both Juliet and I did our best to try and find out who owned the dog that had attacked Penny, causing her so much pain and damage to her body. None of our friends with dogs could recognise our description of the dog concerned, and though we did our best, we were unable to find out the dog's identity, or that of its owners. Our chief worry, and that of our fellow dog-loving friends, was that the dog concerned could suddenly appear and attack another dog, with potentially disastrous results. As it was, Penny had been very lucky to escape with the injuries she'd received. We could only imagine what the result might have been if the attacker had got hold of her by the throat or any area of her head. She could have been killed, or blinded, or ended up losing a limb. The potential list of injuries she could have sustained was quite horrific.

Meanwhile, we did our best to help our little girl to recover from her injuries and the subsequent operation to repair the damage to her body. One thing Penny has always hated is taking tablets of any kind. You would not believe the trouble we have when worming time comes around. We had tried all sorts of methods over the years, but nothing seemed to work, If we hid a tablet in her food, she'd locate it and leave an empty bowl, except for the tablet of course, which would be left in the bowl, as if to say, "I'm not having that horrible thing." We tried crushing the tablets into a powder, which we'd mix with some dog meat and dry food to try fooling her into taking it. No chance! We'd have had more chance of climbing Everest one-legged than trying to get her to take her tablet. She even left it if we added some real human gravy to her food to try and mask the taste of the tablet. It was as if she was psychic, and knew when we were putting 'foreign objects' in her bowl. It wasn't until years later that we finally solved Penny's tablet problem, with...fish!

As part of Sasha's new diet to try and help her to combat her epilepsy, we introduced mackerel and sardines or pilchards to her diet. Penny, by then was much older and showing signs of developing arthritis, so we thought the oily fish, high in Omega 3 oils, might help Penny's joints. When worming time came round again, I had a brainwave.

"Let's try crushing the worming tablet and mixing it in with the fish and lots of the tomato sauce the fish comes in," I suggested. Success! When the fish/sauce/tablet mixture was added to her normal dry food, we'd finally managed to win the battle with Penny's taste buds and her ultra-sensitive nose. Whether it had been taste or smell that had defeated us in the past, we'd finally found the solution to her tablet aversion.

Of course, all this came years after the dog attack, so, there we were, in a position where she had to take a painkiller, which luckily was in liquid form and easily mixed with her food, and, you've guessed it, antibiotic *tablets*, twice a day! We tried the usual methods, mixing in her food etc, all to no avail. Finally, we came up with a novel idea. Hot Dog Sausages. When we went to dog training, we would cut up a can full of hot dogs to use as rewards during the training session. Perhaps they'd work to tempt Penny into taking her tablets. Nice idea, but another failure. She just ate the sausage and spat out the tablets, which weren't even very big. So, as cruel as it sounds, the only way we could get them down her throat was to put the tablet in her mouth, as far back as possible, and then use the small syringe that came with her liquid medicine to squirt water into her mouth and hold her mouth closed until she swallowed. It sounds awful, I know, but it worked, and was the only way we could ensure she received the antibiotics necessary to help prevent any post-operative infection occurring. Thankfully, she only had to take them for five days. It must have been stressful for Penny, and it sure was for us, having to deliver them to her in such a way.

When I took Penny for her first post-operative check-up, the vet was pleased at the progress she was making. She'd been a first-class patient, and even without the dreaded Buster collar, she'd not disturbed her stitches at all, so everything was healing nicely. If she continued to heal at this rate she would be allowed to go for short walks after her next check-up, which would take place in ten days.

During this recovery period, we kept Penny in the lounge during the day, so there was less chance of the other dogs disturbing her or accidentally pulling at her stitches by trying to play with her. So she wouldn't feel too lonely during the daytime, (the rest of our dogs are only allowed in the lounge in the evenings), we allowed little Cassie to join her, thinking she would benefit from the company of another dog. Before we knew it, the two little dogs had gone from being friends, to being *best* friends. Cassie could sense Penny was hurt and instead of doing her usual 'mad ferret' act and bouncing around like a whirling Dervish, trying to encourage Penny to play with her, she became ultra-protective of Penny, almost guarding her like a little mother-hen. If you knew Cassie, you'd know just how surprising her actions were in this instance. Of course, once Penny was fully recovered fully, it was a case of 'normal service' being resumed as far as Cassie was concerned, and Penny would once more become the target for Cassie's exuberance and play. But that was for later. For now, Cassie was the perfect little nurse and companion for Penny.

Wherever Penny went, Cassie was right there with her like

a protective escort, though what tiny Cassie could have done to protect her, it's hard to say. Then again, in her own mind, Cassie probably believes she is as big as any other dog on the street. If you've read Cassie's Tale, you'll know just what I mean. She's one tiny dog with a BIG, BIG attitude. Even then, long before Penny had fully recovered, we made the decision that in future, we'd allow Penny and Cassie to spend the daytimes together in the lounge. They both knew how to ask if they needed to go out for a pee etc, and both would still get their two walks a day, with plenty of time to interact with the rest of the pack.

Recovering with Cassie and Sasha

For now, however, we needed to concentrate on Penny's recovery. When her next Post-op check-up was due, I was over the moon when the vet said she was doing so well that she could now go out for short lead walks, no more than ten minutes at a time, once a day, to begin with. It wasn't much, but in terms of her recovery it represented a massive step for Penny. It was decided that I would take Penny with me for these short walks, and would stay away from the playing fields, both the smaller one near our home, and the larger one where the attack took place. So, every morning, after I'd walked and played with the dogs I took to the small playing field, and after Juliet had finished her walks, I set off with Penny for our short walks, which took us as far as the local church and back home again. Penny was so happy when she saw me holding her lead, as I walked into the lounge that her tail began wagging at top speed, and she did her best to do little jumps of excitement.

She was so happy as we set off down the road and turned on to the lane that led to the church and beyond. Her tail never stopped wagging all the way and despite still being stitched up and looking like Frankenstein's Hound, I could tell she was so proud to be strutting along the lane, doing what dogs love, stopping and sniffing under the bushes that lined the footpath, looking at everyone we passed, (we got a few funny looks from fellow pedestrians), and generally being a normal dog again. As we were on the way back home, a fellow dog walker came towards us and, as they passed us, the lady saw Penny's stitches and asked what had happened to her. I explained what had taken place and she was of course very sympathetic and wished Penny a speedy recovery. Most people we saw however, sort of took one look at my stitched-up dog, and did their best to look the other way. I don't know why. Maybe they found it hard to comment, or were embarrassed at the sight of a dog looking like Penny did. Anyway, Penny was happy as each day we did our little walk and then, when the vet said we could increase her walking time, Juliet started to take her on her regular visits to see her friend.Once a week, Juliet would set off at around 7 p.m. and walk across the large playing field to the houses on the other side, where she'd spend a couple of hours visiting with her best friend, returning around 9.30 p.m. Her friend had a dog called Jet, who got on great with Penny, so she decided to take Penny with her, as she'd done many times in the past. Juliet and her friend could have a good chat, and Penny and Jet would lie together, like two old friends, usually with a bone each to enjoy.

This particular night, Juliet came home at the usual time, but, as she entered through the back gate, and I opened the door to greet her, three of our dogs bounded out with excitement to make their own greetings. In doing so, one of them somehow caught Penny's stitches, probably with their claws or an over-enthusiastic welcome nip, and we were horrified to see blood coming from Penny's wounds.

We could do little that night, but did our best to clean Penny's wounds, and try to stop the bleeding. It didn't need an expert to see that she would need to see the vet first thing in the morning. Sure enough, I was there, waiting when the surgery opened the next day, and the veterinary staff were more than a little surprised to see Penny once again in need of treatment.

Through sheer bad luck and circumstances, her operation wounds had opened up again, especially the flap of skin which was so carefully repaired on the day of the attack. They needed to operate immediately to try and save the skin around that area, as well as clean and re-stitch where other stitches had burst open. Juliet and I faced a worrying few hours as, in a horrible replay of the original injury, poor little Penny was anaesthetised and operated on once again. We felt badly about what had happened, but nobody could have expected that a routine visit to a friend's house, such as Juliet and Penny had carried out many times in the past, would lead to such an awful outcome.

When I called to collect Penny later that day, her vet informed me that she was ok, but that there'd been very little skin to work with as he'd tried to re-join the opened flap of skin. He'd done his best, but had literally had to pull the skin tightly across the wound, which meant that Penny's vulva was now pulled slightly to one side. He assured me it wouldn't affect her ability to pee, but that her vulva was at a slight angle, so when she needed to go to the toilet, the urine stream would go slightly to the side. True enough, ever since that day, every time Penny goes for a pee, it's rather odd to see the stream exiting and shooting off to the left, rather than just going straight for the ground.

We were just glad to get Penny home once again and, of course, now her recovery began all over again, with her bed in the hall, more painkilling and antibiotic medication and no walks until she'd healed sufficiently well, just as before.

6

RUNAWAY, RUNAWAY, RUNAWAY HOME

PENNY'S RESILIENCE and powers of recovery astounded us all, as she quickly went through the next few weeks of post-op checks, various examinations and the usual short walks, gradually progressing to longer ones. Finally, she was given the all-clear by her vet, to return to 'normal' everyday off-lead walks and playtime etc. Throughout her period of convalescence, her appetite had remained perfectly normal, which Bernard the vet agreed had played a big part in her recovery. Some dogs would have suffered a dip in appetite and energy levels after the double trauma she'd undergone, but the fact she'd virtually carried on as normal, eating and drinking as if nothing had happened, contributed greatly to her being able to run and play with our other dogs, and with her friend, Cindy, on the small playing field.

Within a few weeks of the second operation, her body had healed, her fur had almost grown back to cover the scars left by her stitches, and only those who knew her would have guessed at the terrible state she'd been in just a few weeks previously, with blood everywhere and great big gaping holes in her rear end.

It was wonderful to see her once again running and playing normally, chasing her tennis ball and furiously wagging her tail as she enthusiastically raced around the field with the other dogs, who had welcomed her back to their playtimes as if she'd never been away.

Nothing, therefore, could have prepared us for the seemingly innocent little incident which would prove to have a profound effect on Penny and her future playtimes. As I've previously mentioned, she loved it when I threw her ball for her to chase after, pick up and bring back to me, so I could do it all over again. She always looked at her happiest with a tennis ball in her mouth, her tail high up in the air and her little legs flying over the turf of the playing field at top speed.

One day, Penny came back to me with the ball in her mouth as usual, and, as I often did, I went to kick the ball instead of throwing it for her. In what was a total accident, as I kicked the ball on this occasion, instead of it zooming along the grass with Penny pursuing it at top speed, it must have struck a divot or a stone as it seemed to bounce up from the grass and it hit Penny in the face, right on the tip of her snout. Penny squealed, and then, much to my surprise, and Maureen's, who was with me as Cindy played happily with Cassie, she suddenly turned and began to run away from me and the rest of the dogs.

I watched, horrified, as she set off like a bat out of hell, running towards the far side of the field, where the exit, leading to the main road, lay in waiting, complete with cars, lorries, vans, and other road traffic. In my mind, I could visualise disaster looming.

"Penny," I called, "Come here. Penny, be a good girl, come here," I repeated. No response, just the sight of Penny's rear end growing smaller and smaller as she put more and more distance between us. I knew it was useless trying to call her back again. She was clearly in a panic as a result of the ball hitting her in the face, and I grew fearful that she might disappear through the exit and find herself out on the road in just a few seconds. Knowing she had no 'traffic sense,' I was genuinely afraid that she might run in to the road and be knocked down by a passing vehicle. After all she'd gone through already, the thought of losing our little girl, under the wheels of a car, or something even larger, sent a shiver of fear down my spine.

I quickly called the rest of the dogs to me. Obediently, they were all by my side in seconds, and I quickly clipped their leads onto their collars, with one exception. It was time to put Tilly's search and rescue training into operation for real.

"Tilly, go fetch Penny," I ordered, and sure enough, as if she understood every word I said, Tilly set off at full pelt, like an arrow from a bow, straight for where Penny was heading. I hoped that Tilly could overhaul Penny in time to stop her running into the road, and shepherd her back in my direction. Penny now disappeared from sight as she entered the passageway at the far corner of the field which led to the exit. She was now less than thirty yards from the large, green, double gates, one of which was always propped open to allow easy access to the public, there being no logical reason to keep them bolted shut. Tilly, who could run like the wind, was gaining on Penny with every stride, but even so, I had the sinking feeling in my stomach that she wasn't going to make it in time, and, even if she did, would she be able to turn Penny around and stop her running into the road? Tilly was now lost from sight too as she entered the passageway to the exit gates.

With Maureen and Cindy bringing up the rear, I was going as fast as I could, with four dogs on leads running with me, in an attempt to catch up with Tilly, and of course, with Penny, though I knew I was hopelessly outpaced by the two terriers. A few more seconds passed, and then Tilly appeared, coming back towards me. Unfortunately, there was no sign of Penny. I quickly worked out what must have happened. Tilly must have got to the gates, gone through the exit, but Penny must have crossed the road and in her panic, just kept going. Tilly was intelligent enough to know she mustn't try to cross the main road without me, and had sensibly turned around and come back to me. Poor little Tilly; she looked quite disconsolate at having failed in her 'rescue mission' but I gave her a good stroke and a pat, and told her, "Never mind Tilly, you did your best. Good girl."

After clipping Tilly back on her lead, I said my goodbyes to Maureen, who lived in the opposite direction to me and although she offered to help me look for Penny, I told her to go home. I decided to head home with my dogs and get Juliet to help me find the runaway.

As I crossed the road with my dogs, with a sinking feeling in my heart, I suddenly caught sight of a long, wagging tail in the distance. It was Penny, who by now was at the entrance to the street that led to our street, a cul-de-sac just off that avenue. Did Penny have enough sense, that, even in her state of panic, she was heading for home, and safety? Her tail disappeared from sight and within a minute or so, I made the turn onto our street, with Tilly and the other dogs trotting along beside me. When we passed through our garden gate, there was Penny, sitting, waiting at the gate that led to the back door and garden, and, in her mind, sanctuary!

Her tail wagged as I walked up to her. The other dogs all made a fuss of her, as I opened the gate and we all made our way through it into the back garden. I opened the back door to the house and all the dogs, Penny included, trotted into the house as if nothing had happened.

"Had a good time?" Juliet called from the kitchen.

"Not really," I replied, and I proceeded to tell her exactly what had taken place on the playing field.

She was as shocked as I'd been when I first saw Penny 'heading for the hills' after the tennis ball had struck her in the face. "At least we should be grateful she had the sense to find her way home, instead of running off in any old direction and getting lost," she said, eventually.

"Yes," I replied, and then, looking at Penny, "But you were a very naughty girl, running away like that. You should know I would never hurt you on purpose," I said, even though I knew she couldn't really understand me. Penny looked at me, then her head seemed to droop as if she knew she was in trouble. To be honest, I was just so relieved she'd managed to come home unharmed, having crossed the main road without being hit by a car, and then negotiating her way along the streets to find her way to her own home. We were lucky also, that I had the habit of leaving the small front gate to our house open when I took the dogs for a walk, so she was at least able to enter our own property, allowing her to sit on the grass near the large gate leading to our back garden.

Both Juliet and I hoped this would prove to be an isolated incident, but, the following day, when my step-daughter Victoria, who was off school, joined me for my morning walk, Penny looked terrified as soon as I took her tennis ball out of my pocket, her tail drooped to hang between her legs and, if it hadn't been for Victoria quickly clipping her back on her lead, I just knew she'd have bolted for home again. The rest of the dogs who were with us, Tilly, Charlie, Cassie, and Sophie, our lurcher/greyhound cross breed, all continued to enjoy their playtime, especially when

Maureen and Cindy arrived to join us on the field. They happily ran and played with their own balls, but poor Penny seemed to be afraid of the balls, even though they didn't come near her. I'd never seen such a reaction from a dog before. It wasn't as if the tennis ball that struck her had been travelling very fast, and I was sure it couldn't have hurt her, but perhaps the shock of being hit in the face, particularly on her most sensitive organ, her nose, had caused a much deeper traumatic reaction than we could have envisaged.

We stayed for another ten or fifteen minutes, allowing Cindy the opportunity to play and interact with our other dogs, and then reluctantly, left Maureen to complete her walk alone with Cindy as we headed for home.

"You're back early," was Juliet's first reaction when we walked back into the house.

"It's Penny," I replied. "She's absolutely terrified of her ball, and even shied away from the others when they were playing. Victoria had to put her lead on to prevent her from running away again. We didn't want to trust to luck that she'd make it home safely a second time"

"Maybe it would be best if she comes with me on the other field for a while," Juliet suggested. It was a good idea, as when Juliet met up with her dog owning friends on the large field, they never bothered with balls (apart from little Cassie), as the dogs were all allowed to run free and entertain themselves in natural dog play. It was usually a really happy time for the dogs, and their owners could also chat and swap dog stories or the news of the day, and so on.

"Let's try it, and see what happens," I agreed, and so, for the next few days, Penny went with Juliet twice a day. All seemed to calm down and return to normal, until, she happened to see someone else on the field with a ball, not one of our usual dog walk group. Juliet later told me that it took a great effort from her to bring Penny under control and prevent her 'doing a runner' again.

After talking things through, we decided a visit to the vet might be useful so I made an appointment and the next day, Penny and I sat waiting in the surgery for our turn to be seen. The vet was quite shocked when I was able to explain Penny's problem. He admitted he'd never heard of quite such a strong adverse reaction to a minor trauma. Just to be sure, he went out of the consulting room and returned a minute later, holding one hand behind his back.

"Let's see what happens," he said, as he slowly and quietly brought his hand to the front, holding a bright yellow tennis ball. Until a couple of days previously, that would have been Penny's favourite toy in all the world. Now, however, Penny backed away and it was clear to the vet that she had a definite aversion to the sight of the ball. Scratching his head, he looked at Penny, then looked at me, and then came up with a plan.

"Let's try some psychological therapy on Penny. Obviously, she's spent years loving tennis balls and playing with them without any problems. She's had a shock and it's given her a sudden fear of the ball, associating it with something bad happening to her. We need to try and make her realise that the ball is still a fun thing, a toy that gives her pleasure."

"I agree, but how do we go about it?" I asked.

Bernard the vet gave it a little thought and then came up with his idea.

"What is she like with other toys, like soft teddies, chew toys and so on?"

"She'll play with anything soft," I said, "but she's never been bothered much about tug toys and hard plastic toys."

"Okay, for the next week, try getting her to play with anything that isn't ball-shaped. If she's happy then can maybe try introducing a ball to her again and see if she still has a fear of it. It's important we do it while she's playing with other things. Don't let the ball be the only toy on offer. Let her choose. We'll see if having other toys around her will make her forget her fear."

I spent the next few days letting Penny play with a selection of toys and then, after a week, tried Bernard's idea of introducing a tennis ball. At least she didn't run a mile when she saw it, but equally, she completely ignored the ball. I felt really sorry for her. She'd spent her first few years being at her happiest when having a tennis ball to chase and play with, and now it appeared as if one little accident had put an end to her pleasure.

Then, I had another idea. I remembered that when we first met Penny, at Lisa's home, Lisa had thrown that old deflated football for her and Penny had run after it, grabbed it in her jaws and happily run around with it clamped in her mouth. We had a couple of old footballs in the shed, that Tilly and Charlie liked to play with in the garden, so, one afternoon, I took Penny into the back garden on her own, having already placed one of the footballs on the ground in readiness. Penny didn't appear to show any fear of it, and when I rolled it slowly towards her, she made no attempt to run away from it, though she didn't try to pick it up or play with it. Over the next half hour, I persevered with her and gradually she came round to the idea that there was some fun to be had. Eventually, she decided to touch the ball, tentatively pushing it a short distance with her nose.

"Good girl, Penny," I said, enthusiastically, encouraging her to do it again by rolling the soft, deflated ball towards her. As if by a small miracle, her tail began to wag and at last, she plucked up the courage to grasp it between her teeth. To my great surprise and pleasure, she began to run around the garden with the big, soft football in her mouth. It wasn't her usual tennis ball, but at least we'd found a ball of sorts she could and would, play with.

I phoned the vet's surgery and spoke to Bernard who was happy with her progress. He encouraged me to continue with the 'therapy,' hoping we might eventually find a way to get Penny reunited with her tennis ball.

Sadly, as the weeks passed, it became clear that Penny was never going to enjoy playing with a tennis ball again. Something had 'clicked' in her mind and from that time to the present day, Penny lost her love of playing with tennis balls, though a deflated football was acceptable to her.

Isn't it strange how something as innocuous as that one small accident with her tennis ball could have such a lasting psychological effect on a dog? At least, there were lots of other toys she could play with, and she gradually accepted the presence of tennis balls when the other dogs were playing with them, though we took care to make sure the balls never got too close to Penny. So, there we were, having to accept that our lovely little girl had a psychological hang-up. Once again, we'd learned a valuable lesson in canine psychology and the way a dog's mind can work.

Penny, Tilly and Frisbee

One day, a friend gave Tilly a frisbee to play with. On one occasion when I took it with us on the playing field to throw for Tilly to play with, I was astounded when, having thrown it a couple of times for Tilly, I did it again, and Penny suddenly took off in hot pursuit of the frisbee. She gathered it up in her mouth before Tilly could retrieve it, and began prancing around, proudly holding the thing up in the air, sticking out from one side of her mouth, being careful not to trip over it as she ran. Purely by chance, we'd found a new toy that Penny loved to play with and from that day, we always took the frisbee with us on Penny's walk. l was so happy for our little dog. She'd found a new favourite toy and all the bad thoughts about her experience with the tennis ball incident seemed to have been finally put behind us.

7

SEA MONSTERS IN SCARBOROUGH!

NO MATTER what had happened in her life, Penny always came across as being happy and contented. Even the dog attack quickly faded from her memory, as far as we could tell, and she was soon her normal self again, showing no fear of other dogs that might approach her. Her tail would wag and she was always happy to make new 'doggie' friends.

One nice, bright and sunny autumn day, we decided to visit Juliet's two oldest children (both adults by now), who lived and worked in Scarborough, on the east coast, a hugely popular holiday resort. With it being a warm, sunny day, we decided to take a couple of the dogs with us, so we decided to take Dylan and Penny. They were both small and good travellers in the car, (we thought), so were ideal for a day at the seaside.

The journey was a nightmare. Juliet and I were in the front of the car, Rebecca and Victoria in the back and the two dogs in the rear of the estate car. We stopped at a rest point about halfway through our journey of round about 80 miles, to let the dogs out for a walkabout, and to go to the toilet. Opening the tailgate, we discovered that one of the dogs had been sick. Was it Penny or Dylan? As Dylan had travelled many times in the car, we guessed that Penny had to be the culprit. The second half of the journey saw me pulling over at least five times, as Penny continued vomiting every few minutes. Each time we let her out of the car, she ran to the grass verge beside the road to try and eat grass, and if she peed once, she must have done so at least a dozen times during that awful last few miles. We assumed that the trauma of her operations must have altered Penny's psyche in some way. She'd travelled in the car on numerous occasions and this was the first time she'd exhibited such behaviour.

We finally arrived at our destination and our first stop was at the farm owned and operated as a livery yard by Juliet's friend, Sheila, her best friend from the time she lived in the resort herself.

The dogs loved walking around on the farm, all the new sights and smells must have been heavenly to their doggie senses. Dylan in particular loved walking along the lane that led from the livery stable to the road, seeing the horses in the fields, and I loved the commanding views that the walk afforded me from the farm's setting, high above the town itself. He and I enjoyed a lovely, peaceful walk, taking in all the sights, sounds and smells of the countryside. Even though Scarborough is a fairly large seaside resort town, it is surrounded by the beautiful countryside of the North Yorkshire Moors, a National Park with many beautiful villages and areas of open country and forestry to explore. The countryside begins within a couple of miles of the outskirts of the town.

Penny, however, barked almost non-stop and tried her best to chase the horses, much to our surprise. Penny had been brought up in close proximity to Lisa's two horses, without causing a problem. There were quite often horses on the rough scrubland that bordered the large playing field at home, and Penny had never once made any attempt to chase or disturb them. Maybe the sea air was playing havoc with her senses. Was it the strange smells of the farm, or the fact she'd suffered from an upset tummy on the journey that were causing her unusual behaviour? Whatever the reason, we felt compelled to put her back on her lead and she spent the rest of the time at the farm under close supervision. Penny was in disgrace!

After staying long enough to sit and have a coffee and a good long chat with Sheila, we left the farm and made our way into town to visit Juliet's son and daughter from her first marriage. They'd both managed to take some time off work to spend with us, and it was so nice for Juliet to get to share some time with them.

Both dogs were loving their day out, and the sea air was doing us all a power of good. Penny was her usual self again once we left the farm, and there was no repeat of her earlier sickness as we drove into the town and headed for the sea front, luckily finding a parking space within a few yards of the beach. During the summer, dogs are banned from the beach at Scarborough, but, luckily for us, the official tourist season had just ended and we were able to take them both for a great walk and to play on the sands. It was obviously the first time either dog had felt the sensation of sand under their paws, as both were a little tentative at first, when they felt the warm softness of the beach beneath their feet, but soon got used to it and began to enjoy themselves.

We started our walk at one end of the beach, which began beside one side of the harbour wall. Scarborough's harbour is a busy port, being home to a small fleet of trawlers, as well as a number of popular pleasure 'steamers' which provide tourists and holidaymakers with trips along the coast. Still referred to as steamers, these vessels are nowadays powered by modern diesel engines and no longer send plumes of smoke into the air from their funnels as they sail along.

For those who don't know Scarborough well, or at all, I should mention that it is one of England's most popular holiday resorts. Situated on the east coast, it has two bays, both with sandy beaches, which are split by a headland, on top of which stand the ruins of the 12th century Scarborough Castle, commissioned by King Henry II, and an important Royal fortification in guarding England's East coast against invaders from Scandinavia. The stone castle, built by Henry, replaced an earlier wooden fortification built by William le Gros, a powerful Anglo-Norman baron, a grand-nephew of William the Conqueror. The castle was even shelled by a German Naval bombardment on 16th December 1914 when two German battleships, the *Derfflinger* and *Von der Tann*, fired more than 55 shells into the town and castle from Scarborough Bay, also striking the lighthouse and causing so much damage to the tower that it had to be pulled down. Thankfully it was eventually rebuilt. Eighteen of the town's civilian population were killed during the bombardment.

Apart from the castle, the town also boasts a Sea Life Centre, which houses Yorkshire's only seal hospital and the world-renowned Peasholm Park, an oriental themed municipal park which even includes its own naval battle as one of its attractions, fought by remote controlled model warships, and a new, ultra-modern holiday complex, *The Sands,* managed by Juliet's daughter, Rachel, and son Robert, situated right on the sea front, with stunning views over the sea. Since she's grown up, my youngest step-daughter, Victoria, has joined them, and now lives and works in Scarborough too, where she's learning the hospitality trade under the auspices of Rachel and Robert and where she also helps to take care of their dogs in her off-duty hours. She loves to come home regularly in her shiny new car, mostly to see the dogs, rather than her Mum and me. Sheba has always been special to Victoria, and when she was growing up, our little rescued Staffy, a former bait dog, severely abused by dog fighters, used to sleep in Victoria's bedroom. Sheba had her own bed in the room, but very often, if Juliet or I peeped into the room before we turned in for the night, we'd see Sheba and Victoria, beautifully snuggled up in Victoria's bed, Victoria's arm usually draped across Sheba, keeping her safe and secure. Only later, when Victoria was in her teens, did Sheba begin to sleep downstairs again, as Victoria would often be out with her friends at night. The dog's bedtime would come before she arrived home, so it was no longer practical for Sheba to share her room, especially if she had a friend sleeping over. Whenever she comes home for a visit, Victoria always makes a big fuss of Sheba, and the other dogs of course, but there's no denying that there is a special bond between the two of them.

Victoria with Sheba and Penny

SCARBOROUGH IS ALSO home to one of the country's oldest operational lifeboat stations, standing on the north pier, which is a popular visitor attraction in its own right. And now, let's return to our walk on the beach.

As I mentioned earlier, we began our walk beside the harbour wall, which also served as a wide promenade where people could sit and watch the world go by. From here people can see the ships entering or leaving the harbour, or perhaps sit on one of the benches provided, or on the wall itself and eat their fish and chips, bought from one of many nearby Fish and Chip shops, serving freshly cooked, locally caught fish, mostly tasty cod or haddock. The presence of those enjoying their fish meals, and the newly docked trawlers also served to attract many seagulls that wheeled, screeched and swooped like a squadron of feathered dive bombers, often landing close enough for people to throw them a few scraps from their meal. Others landed on the beach and began pecking at the sand, presumably seeking some tasty morsel or two, shellfish or worms perhaps, buried in the sand, waiting for the coming of the next high tide.

On the beach

Dylan and Penny were attracted by the screeching and squawking of the gulls as they dived and swooped overhead. Penny decided to do her best to ignore them, or perhaps to imitate them, as she began to sniff at the sand and then started to use her front paws to start digging a nice hole in the beach.

We laughed, wondering what on earth she was trying to achieve. Whatever it was, she was enjoying herself, and that was all that mattered. Dylan, on the other hand, had higher thoughts in mind. By that comment, I really do mean *higher*. His attention was firmly fixed on the seagulls. This being his first visit to the coast, he'd obviously never seen or heard seagulls before. These very large flying monsters were nothing like the little sparrows and starlings that regularly visited the bird tables in our garden, where we daily place food for our local bird population. Oh no, these grey and white things that now flew and sometimes hovered above us must have seemed like beasts from another world to our little Bedlington terrier. The one thing I have to say about Dylan is that he is incredibly brave, can run like a greyhound and leap like a gazelle.

Before we knew what was happening, he must have made his doggie mind up, and decided these large flying monsters were a threat that needed dealing with. Much to our amusement he began leaping into the air, trying to catch the squadron of gulls that zoomed around above our heads. As one flew away, he'd turn his attention to another one and he would run and chase the next one in their formation, doing his best to catch one. As they had the advantage of flight, and were mostly at least twenty or thirty feet above him, he had no chance, but we couldn't really tell Dylan that, could we? He was having great fun trying! Juliet then caught my attention and told me to look up at the harbour wall.

A small crowd of holidaymakers, (and maybe some locals) had gathered to watch Dylan in his comical attempt to catch himself a seagull. The laughter was now easily heard from our position on the beach and of course, we could share in their amusement as they looked and pointed and even beckoned others to come and watch the little dog in his futile battle with the gulls. Rebecca and Victoria thought it was hilarious and everyone was clearly enjoying 'The Dylan Show' as he carried on for at least five minutes until a mixture of tiredness and boredom at his failure to catch a seagull probably signalled the end of his brave quest. That, plus the fact that most of the gulls had flown away, obviously seeking richer pickings further along the beach. When Dylan finally gave up his efforts, we were astounded when the sound of laughter from the harbour wall turned into a round of applause from some of those who'd enjoyed watching him. People shouted things like, "Better luck next time, fella," and "You need longer legs," and "Good try, young' un." We acknowledged the laughter and comments by waving to everyone, receiving many waves and blown kisses, (hopefully for Dylan), in return.

As we turned to continue our walk along the beach we waved once more to the happy throng on the wall. Some of them, especially those who may have been on a day trip to the seaside, as we were, would probably remember the crazy little dog that looked like a sheep cavorting around, chasing seagulls, for some time after they returned home that night.

It was only as we began walking away, proceeding further along the beach that I realised my cheeks were aching. I'd laughed so much myself, and Dylan had certainly enjoyed himself. Penny on the other hand, looked at us all as if we'd all gone mad. She'd succeeded in digging a couple of nice deep holes in the sand, and had certainly enjoyed herself as much as Dylan had. Due to the possibility of him running off and trying to continue his seagull hunt, we kept Dylan on his lead as we progressed along the beach, but Penny was running free and seemed to have completely recovered from her upsetting car journey. We weren't really mad at her for her behaviour on the farm, as she was clearly excited and overwhelmed by the sight of so many horses in one place. We also knew she was just being playful and would never have tried to hurt the horses. Such a thing simply wasn't in her nature.

Now, however, it was her turn for some fun. Bearing in mind the fact that she'd never seen the sea before, we were surprised when she began approaching the whitecaps that were gently breaking as they reached the beach. Penny seemed intrigued by them and then, she tentatively padded right up to the water's edge and dipped one of her front paws in the sea. Now, at any time of the year, the waters of the North Sea are definitely on the cold side, but Penny appeared unfazed by the water temperature as she slowly began to walk into the waves. Before we knew it, she was having the time of her life, jumping and splashing around in the sea. She wore a look of pure delight on her little face, and we laughed again as we saw how much she was enjoying herself. While this was taking place, Juliet walked Dylan closer to the water's edge, and tried to encourage him to have a paddle in the sea. There was more laughter as Dylan sort of dipped the end of one paw in the water, and then leaped back in shock, presumably from the cold temperature of the water, or maybe from the fact it was moving. Did he think it was some kind of giant monster?

Speaking of monsters, we now looked towards Penny, who was still in the sea, having a 'whale of a time,' (pardon the pun). She'd gone further out into the waves and for a moment, I was worried in case she got caught by the current and pulled out to sea. Suddenly, a larger wave approached the beach and for a few seconds, Penny disappeared beneath the white capped surf. Then, like a little sea monster rising from the deep, her head appeared, and, with a look of total enjoyment on her face, she powered her way up through the surf and headed towards us as we stood watching her in amazement. She was completely at home in the sea, and as she finally emerged, dripping from her swim in the ocean, she gave an almighty shake, soaking most of us, and wagged her tail which produced a constantly swerving spray of seawater as she shook out the sea from her rear appendage.

Sea monster!

"I think she's enjoyed that," Juliet said with a big smile on her face.

"I think you're right," I replied, "but we don't have a towel to dry her with, do we?"

We hadn't come prepared for either of the dogs to go swimming in the sea, so for the next half hour or so we carried on our walk in the afternoon sunshine, as Penny gradually dried off. Dylan, who'd eventually managed a sort of paddle in the shallowest of breaking waves, was hardly wet and his paws dried in no time.

By the time Penny had dried out, it was nearing the time

for us to head for home, where my friend, Ken had kindly spent the day dog-sitting our other dogs. They'd all be wondering where we were. So, leaving the beach, and realising we were all hungry, we called at the nearest fish and chip shop, and bought ourselves some real seaside fish and chips, which we sat on the sea wall and ate, before heading to the car park. We were thankfully not bothered by any ravenous, roving seagulls as we ate, so were spared the sight of Dylan trying to take off into the Scarborough sky in his attempts to catch one.

I drove especially carefully on the way home, in an attempt to prevent a repeat of the morning journey, with Penny being sick during the ride. We had an idea that the movement was felt more violently in the rear of the car, so this time, we put Penny in the front foot well, between Juliet's feet, and, miraculously, it did the trick. The extra stability and security she felt must have helped to settle Penny's stomach, and of course, she was probably tired out by her oceanic exertions at the beach, so she slept most of the way home.

We were of course greeted like long lost best friends by the rest of the dogs on our return, and after feeding them all and saying thank you to Ken, who left for home, we were able to settle down together for the evening. All the dogs were soon snoozing peacefully, and Penny and Dylan, who were especially tired, were the first of the pack to be snoring happily.

Our day at the seaside had been a happy and enjoyable one, and the mental picture of Penny, our very own sea monster, emerging triumphantly from the waves, lives with me to this day, so much so that we had a canvas made of her triumphant emergence from the sea.

A final paddle

8

STICKS!

PENNY WAS GROWING OLDER and the members of our little pack were growing older with her. We'd introduced some new members to our little family as others had sadly left us and when we brought home two sisters and a brother, from a single litter, Petal, Muffin and Digby, our family seemed complete again. The three puppies were only eight weeks old when we first saw them, and for once, these babies were not strictly rescues. We'd recently lost a young dog, Chudleigh, who'd been very special to Juliet, and sadly, she became very down and depressed at his loss. I knew she needed a new focus and, though we know you can never replace a dog that holds a place in your heart, I felt that Juliet needed a new pup to provide it.

I'd told her to keep an eye out in the local press for dog adverts, and one day she told me she'd seen an advertisement for a litter of Staffy/Springer Spaniel crosses. I agreed we'd look into it, (no promises made), and I phoned the number quoted in the paper. The lady I spoke to told me they had five puppies, as well as the mother and father, so we were welcome to go and see them, and meet both parents too.

I arranged for me and Juliet to visit them the following day. The people only lived about three or four miles away so it wouldn't take long to get there. Leaving the girls at home to look after the dogs, (it was half-term, so no school), we arrived at the address we'd been given at around ten thirty on a nice, unusually warm, October morning. We were greeted by a lovely couple, whom we warmed to right away. They led us into the lounge where we were introduced to the dog parents. The father was a white Staffordshire Bull Terrier and the mother, a black and tan springer spaniel. Both dogs welcomed us with wagging tails and were definitely people-friendly, as they both made a big fuss of us.

"We thought you'd like to meet the parents first," the lady said. "You can see what lovely temperaments they both have."

"That was very thoughtful of you," I replied. "It's always good if you can see one or both parents when buying a puppy."

"You'd better come and meet the pups now," she said as she and her husband both led the way to their kitchen, where in seconds, we were 'assaulted' by five tiny bundles of fur, tails wagging furiously as they fought for our attention, clambering over each other in the way that puppies do.

The lady explained that the smallest of the pups would be staying with them as it was quite weak and they wouldn't like to sell it to anyone, and their son was taking another one, which left us three to choose from. Juliet and I both had different preferences, but I allowed her to make the choice, a little black puppy with a white flash, which she said she'd call Muffin. We arranged to pick her up the next day, as we needed to buy various things before we could take her home. That night, Juliet wasn't sure if she'd made the right choice, but I assured her she had, though I'd secretly devised a special surprise for her. Next morning, while she was in the bath, I quietly phoned the lady we were buying the puppy from and made a clandestine arrangement. Later in the morning, when I left to collect Muffin, I returned with not one, but TWO puppies. I'd also bought the black and white one and when I walked into the house carrying both little pups, one in each arm, Juliet's face lit up, a pure picture! Because of the shape of her markings, we soon named our second puppy, Petal. Both she and Muffin quickly settled in, being 'mothered' by our lovely Sasha, who seemed to have appointed herself as the puppies' surrogate mother, keeping the puppies close to her at all times, and letting them cuddle up to sleep with her at night. After a couple of weeks, we received a phone call from the lady who'd sold us the sisters, asking if we would like the last pup in the litter. She explained that they'd had a buyer for the little male dog, and John, her husband had agreed to deliver it, but when he arrived at the address they'd been given, the place looked awful, almost a hovel, and he refused to hand over the puppy. They had talked it over and, remembering how much we'd loved all the puppies, immediately thought of us. They were happy to accept a greatly reduced price, just so the little dog could go to a good home, so Juliet and I quickly discussed it and I phoned them back to say I'd be with them in half an hour. So, soon after, Muffin and Petal were reunited with their brother, a brindle and white little boy, who we named Digby. Three puppies to raise at once, proved less trouble than having a single pup, as they seemed to learn from each other, and soon settled in to our little pack, and its daily routine, helped of course by their new 'mum', Sasha.

Penny, by now one of our senior pack members, accepted the three newcomers immediately. She of course sensed they were just babies, and when they had completed their course of inoculations, and were able to go for walks, Penny often joined them in those early days. Walking with an older, more experienced dog like Penny, helped the puppies to learn the things they could and couldn't do in company with the dogs they'd meet on the playing field. It was around this time that Sasha exhibited her first epileptic seizures, and so she was unable to 'go walkies' with the puppies, as she was under some very strong medication at the time and was reduced to lead walks only for a while.

The puppies, Muffin, Digby, Petal, ten weeks old

Very soon, the puppies were well trained and, being younger and faster, they no longer needed slower, older Penny to accompany them on their walks and playtimes, so, Penny was back with me and my little 'crew' on the smaller playing field, where she could run and play at her own speed, with our other older dogs, and with Cindy.

After the problems we'd had finding suitable toys that

Penny would accept and play with, I was surprised to see, one day, Penny return from rummaging around under the bushes with a long, thick stick in her mouth. It must have been at least two feet long and was still so fresh that it had a number of green leaves still attached to it. Penny looked immensely proud of herself as she came running up to me with the stick, (it was actually a broken branch from one of the bushes that surround the field), which she happily dropped at my feet, tail up in the air, and a look on her face that seemed to say, "Well, are you going to throw it for me, or what?"

What else could I do? Penny looked so pleased with herself and I dutifully picked up her stick and threw it for her. She didn't hesitate. Off she went, happily running after the stick, picking it up and bringing it back, a little unbalanced, as it was longer on one side than the other from the way she'd picked it up, once again dropping it at my feet. I was quite amazed, as in all the years she'd been with us, Penny had never shown any inclination or desire to play with sticks. Obviously, things had changed. When the walk was over, Penny insisted on taking her new 'treasure' with her and proudly trotted home with the stick proudly carried in her mouth, occasionally banging into one of the other dogs who were trying to walk beside her. Penny couldn't have cared less. She was happy!

Once again, our little 'railway pup' had managed to surprise us. Juliet was as surprised as I'd been when we arrived home. I wouldn't allow Penny to bring the stick into the house, so she simply stayed outside in the garden, lying on her tummy, gnawing at her stick. Very soon, there wasn't much left of her new prized possession and I was forced to take the remains from her and throw it in the bin. The look she gave me!!!

"Don't worry, Penny. I'm sure we can find you another one when we go on the field again. If a dog could sulk, I'd swear that

Penny spent the next hour or so, doing just that, until feeding time came around, and at last, her focus turned to more important things...food.

Sure enough, the next day, when we arrived on the playing field, Penny made a bee-line for the bushes, obviously looking for another stick. She soon returned with one, luckily a smaller, easier to throw version of the one she'd previously found. I could only guess that perhaps some older children or teenagers had broken some of the branches off the various bushes. The ones that she'd found so far were what I think are termed 'green' as they were still fresh and it was obvious that they'd been deliberately broken off from the living bushes. I've never condoned vandalism in any shape or form, but at least, in this case, Penny was gaining something from it.

As time went on, Penny definitely proved that, despite her age, (by this time she was over ten years old), she still had plenty of energy and the will to play and enjoy herself. As winter approached and the bushes died back, the supply of sticks for her to play with increased as some of the bushes died back and lots of 'new' sticks became available for her to enjoy. Funnily enough, although it seems to be an accepted thing that dogs like to play with sticks, only one of our other dogs showed any interest in them. Dexter would occasionally join me on my playing field walk, and, like Penny, he enjoyed rummaging around in the bushes that grew around the borders of the field. On a number of occasions, he too would emerge with a stick, and would play with it for a few minutes before becoming bored with it and literally dumping it where it fell. Any attempt by me, Victoria or Maureen, if she was with us, to get him to run and fetch the stick after he'd grown bored with it, met with stubborn resistance as he'd just look the other way, or, more usually, just wander off to explore another area of the field. Dexter never wanted to carry a stick home or spend more than about ten minutes playing with or chasing one. We did find he was quite clever in one respect though. When we were about to leave for home, I'd pick up any stick he'd been playing with and would place it under a bush. Quite often, when we next returned to the field, Dexter would wander off and after a few minutes, reappear from the bushes carrying 'his' stick. He can be quite clever when he wants to be, our Dexter, though, as I write this, he's been spending a lot of time at the vet.

Poor Dexter is sadly growing old, and although he's been one of the fittest and healthiest dogs we've ever owned, he has begun to show signs of not being well in the last year. Most recently, he's developed a very bad cough, and after tests and examinations, he's been found to have a heart condition, fluid on his lungs, which are now only operating at 30 – 40% capacity, and anaemia. He's been with us for over 11 years, and when we adopted him, we learned that he'd been thrown from a car travelling at high speed on a motorway, and had been very lucky to survive. He's a real laid-back soul who is simply suffering from the symptoms of old age.

Dexter

But, back to his younger days, and as I was saying, he was quite the 'retriever' in his day. I forgot to say he's part Labrador and part Staffy, a crossbreed that is very popular in Spain, I've learned, where they are known as 'Staffadors.' His time on the playing field was always pleasurable as he was no trouble to take out and was the doggie equivalent of a perfect gentleman. It was quite something to see him disappear under the bushes and a couple of minutes later, see him emerge triumphantly with his tail wagging and his stick in his mouth. Nowadays we call him the 'bird dog,' as he likes to spend most of his time sitting or lying in the sun under the bird table at the bottom of the garden, where sparrows, starlings and other birdie visitors to our garden are so used to him that they flock around him and hop and peck around on the ground all around him, totally unafraid of him. He never bothers them and likes to watch them feeding up on the bird table when I put the food out for them in the morning. It's true to say that both Dexter and Penny have incredibly mild temperaments and wouldn't hurt a fly.

Now that Penny had found her love of stick play, we were constantly on the lookout for suitable sticks for her to play with. We're not exactly surrounded by trees where we live so mostly the sticks we found were small pieces of broken off branches of the bushes that lined the borders of the playing fields and some roadside areas. As winter slowly began to take autumn's place in the calendar, and the days grew shorter and the nights grew longer, we knew the supply of 'Penny Sticks' would gradually diminish, so, we began to create a little stockpile of sticks in our garden shed. Whenever any of us found a suitable toy for Penny while we were out and about, it would be brought home and added to the collection until, at one point, anyone looking into our shed might have been forgiven for imagining we were planning on building our own version of a beaver dam.

Eventually, I decided enough was enough. We had enough sticks to last Penny for a year or more and I called time on the stick scavenging. Very soon, the afternoons were so short of daylight that our afternoon playtimes with the dogs grew shorter, along with the dwindling afternoon light, and soon, with winter upon us, most of our afternoon walks were lead walks, as it wasn't possible to let the dogs run around and play on the dark playing fields. Sometimes, we'd manage to get out early, so some of them could take advantage of the shrinking daylight but that became more of a rarity as winter took its full hold over the country. It was that time of year when nature itself seemed to hold its breath as it waited for the snow, the rain, the ice and gales to relent with the coming of a new year and the advent of another spring, when the land appeared reborn once more, and we could enjoy the return of warmer days.

9

THE STATELY HOME (LADY PENELOPE)

PENNY WAS AGEING GRACEFULLY. To look at her, you would have had difficulty telling the senior dog she'd now become from the young dog we'd adopted all those years ago. People had always thought she was an old dog, even when she'd been no more than a puppy. The white hair, mixed in to her black facial markings obviously gave everyone that impression. Even Juliet and I were amazed that she wasn't really showing any signs of further ageing. Her tail wagged as fiercely as ever when she was excited, and in fact, I christened her the 'little drummer girl' because her tail, which is quite thick and long, is actually very loud if it comes into contact with, for example, the washing machine as she waits to have her lead put on before a walk. As for feeding time, well, she lies on her tummy in the hallway with Cassie, as they wait patiently for their food. In Penny's case, she lies close to the wall, and the noise of her tail swiping the wall as she wags it back and forth with excitement and anticipation is very much like the sound of someone striking a big bass drum.

But I'm digressing from the point of this chapter here, so do forgive me. What I want to talk about here is Penny's day out at a local stately home. Standing about ten miles from our home is Cusworth Hall, once the home of the influential Battie-Wrightson family, and known as the jewel in Doncaster's crown. The 18th century Grade1 listed building with its adjoining gardens and country park remained, unusually for such large manor houses, in the family ownership until 1952 when death duties and taxes on the death of Robert Cecil Battie-Wrightson, forced the sale of its contents by its last owner, Mrs. Maureen Pearce, who subsequently sold the hall to Doncaster Council. Over the years, the council has turned the hall into a major tourist attraction, with a superb museum within the hall itself and magnificent landscaped gardens, all freely accessible to the public. The sloping gardens and enormous lawned area to the rear of the hall lead down to a lake at the bottom of the hill, upon which swans, ducks and other aquatic birds are found.

The reason I mention all this is that the grounds have become a Mecca for families and dog walkers, especially in the summer months, and it was here that we decided, one day, to take Penny and a couple of our other dogs for an afternoon out. It was a beautiful sunny day, only a few cotton-wool clouds hung in the sky above the hall and its grounds as we parked the car in the car park. The four of us, plus four dogs, exited the vehicle and made our way along the tree-lined footpath towards the rear of the country house and the beautiful, lush, grassed embankment that led down to the lake. There were a couple of large areas where trees had been planted, many years ago, presumably to act as windbreaks for the family as they enjoyed their own private walks in the direction of the lake, where benches have been added to allow today's visitors to rest and enjoy watching the wildlife on the lake. I would imagine that the Battie-Wrightsons would have also provided themselves with seating around or close to the lake, such items clearly long gone in the modern era.

Now though, it was our turn, along with other like-minded families, to take advantage of the grounds of the Hall, and we were soon enjoying the afternoon sunshine, along with Penny, Muttley, Tilly and Cassie. After wandering around the grounds, close to the Hall itself, we began to make our way down the grassy slope towards the lake. Arriving at the water's edge, we followed the path around the lake, stopping now and then to watch, first, a little family of moorhens as they made their way towards one of the two small islands that stood, one at each end of the lake, and then, a beautiful black swan as it made its solitary progress along the length of the man-made waterway. The dogs didn't seem to be bothered by the moorhens, but were a little suspicious of the beautiful black swan as it glided past the place where we stood, turning its head and looking imperiously in our direction. On the far side of the lake, we saw its mate, which began gliding in our direction to meet up with its partner. We slowly made our way all around the lakeside path, stopping once for a five-minute rest on one of the benches. As Juliet and I sat, enjoying the warmth of the sun for those few minutes, the girls led the dogs, two apiece, back towards the grass of the sloping grounds, then we saw them enjoying themselves as the dogs joined Rebecca and Victoria in a race back towards us, down the grassy slope. The dogs were on their leads, so it ended in a six-way draw, as they all arrived back where we were sitting at the same time, the girls laughing, each claiming they'd won, while the dogs wagged their tails and panted from their efforts. Luckily, we'd come prepared. Juliet took a water bottle and a small bowl from her shoulder bag, and gave them all a drink before we resumed our walk around the lake. We finally made our way back, negotiating the uphill climb towards the main grounds and the Hall, where we could allow the dogs off their leads for a bit of a run. They weren't allowed off-lead in the lake area in case they disturbed the birds that lived on and around the water. Penny emerged from the trees with a discarded plastic bottle in her mouth, and set to work, enjoying playing with it for a few minutes.

Penny's bottle

By the time they'd had fifteen or twenty minutes off-lead, with the girls playing a game that resembled hide-and-seek around the trees with them, the dogs had tired themselves out and were happy to come and lie down. They snoozed on the grass as we all sat down, enjoying the views, which, from where we sat, included a marvellous, panoramic view of the whole town of Doncaster and beyond, truly a sight worth seeing.

We were about to bring our afternoon in the sun to an end, when a lady walked along with a pair of Yorkshire Terriers beside her. Our dogs became excited and, before long, the friendly Yorkies and our dogs were enjoying a game of 'tag' as they chased one another around, with barks and 'yaps' of excitement adding sound effects to their fun. After a few minutes of this frantic exertion, the dogs seemed to tire of the game and before long, after saying goodbye to the lady and her dogs, we were once again on our way through the tree-lined path towards the car park.

As we climbed back into the car, Juliet had an idea.

"It's still nice and warm. It's too soon to go home. Why don't we call at the garden centre before we call it a day?"

"Good idea," I replied. The garden centre she referred to was only a mile away, and with a large outdoor area as well as indoor facilities, it would be a nice way to end our day out where the dogs could enjoy a leisurely walk around the place with us. It also happened to be right next door to a lovely pub, where we might have time to enjoy a drink before heading home.

We enjoyed our visit to the garden centre and even bought a couple of plants for our garden, and then, leaving the dogs to snooze in the car, we walked across the car park to the pub, where we spent a leisurely few minutes enjoying a drink together. Finally we decided to head for home as the other dogs would surely be missing us by now.

We were home in a short time, and sure enough, we were welcomed home by our other dogs, who behaved as though we'd been away for weeks, rather than a couple of hours. The first priority on arriving home was to let them all out in the garden, and then it was feeding time. Our absence certainly hadn't affected anyone's appetite, and after tea, we took it in turns to take them all out for short walks, except those who'd been to Cusworth of course.

The day had been a welcome distraction for us all and, as

we settled down to watch a couple of hours of TV, the dogs joined us in the lounge, taking up various spaces on the sofa with Juliet, on my armchair, and a couple even using the dog beds on the floor. It wasn't long before our evening's television entertainment was being serenaded by numerous dog snores of contentment. I think both Juliet and I fell asleep while watching a movie, with Sasha, (the loudest snorer), draped across my lap, and Juliet almost buried beneath the combined weight and presence of Digby, Muffin, Petal and Sheba. Our lounge became a perfect haven of peace and tranquillity, only disturbed when we woke up in time to put the dogs out for the last time that day, before heading off to bed.

Another happy day out was over and we vowed to repeat the visit to Cusworth again soon, taking a different group of dogs with us, which we did, quite often after that day, as the country park became one of our favourite destinations for doggie days out until the coming of colder weather. We loved it, our dogs loved it, but the cold weather made it less enjoyable so we put those visits on hold until the following year, and the anticipated warmer days of springtime.

Meanwhile, the inexorable march of winter slowly forced autumn into the background and what I like to call 'the shivering season' was upon us in no time. Dogs, having fur coats, tend to be less susceptible to the cold than we poor, weak humans, but even so, thousands of years of domestication have rendered many of today's pet canines quite unable to stand the cold to any great degree. Every year, I also hear tales of dogs being left outside in freezing cold weather, and sadly, many poor dogs die as a result of what I can only describe as wilful neglect by their unthinking and unfeeling owners, literally frozen to death in the snow and ice of a bitter winter.

Thankfully, nobody I know would treat their pets that way, and in fact the whole meaning of the word 'pet' when applied to a dog, speaks to me of a member of the family, one who shares the home and the life of their owner, not a 'thing' to be kept outdoors in all weathers and left to suffer in a freezing kennel or worse during the ravages of winter. Even working dogs, kept as guard dogs for example, need warmth and comfort in the depths of winter, otherwise, how can they be expected to fulfil their role of protecting their owner's property?

Of course, for Penny and the rest of our pack, our home is their home, and, fur coats or not, nearly all of them have warm dog coats which they wear when out on their winter walks. I say 'nearly all' because a couple of them simply refuse to wear a dog coat and prefer to go 'au naturel' when they go for walks, no matter what the weather. The one exception to the wearing of their coats however, is when one of our dogs' favourite events takes place...SNOW!

I think it's safe for me to say that all our dogs absolutely love romping and playing in the snow. It's a joy to watch them cavorting around, chasing each other, rolling over and over and generally having a great time in the soft, white snows of winter. Those with shorter fur don't present too much of a problem when they come home, and can soon be towelled dry once we're back indoors. Unfortunately, three of our dogs have longer fur, so Penny, Dylan and Cassie have a problem that doesn't really affect the others, namely snow-fur balls!

After a few minutes of running and playing in the snow, their legs and undersides tend to be covered in balls of snow that quickly turn to ice and, if not removed properly on returning home, can cause serious problems for the dogs. Having such short legs, Penny is usually the worst affected of our dogs, so, after she's had a great time playing in the snow, we have to carefully remove the snow and ice from her fur and especially from her paws. A nice bowl of warm, (not hot) water soon helps to thaw any ice balls that have formed on her paws, and either a nice warm towel, or a hair dryer on a low setting, helps to melt and remove the snow that clings to her tummy, chest and the rest of her body. We use the same method on Dylan and Cassie and before long, they are all clear of the ice and back to normal again.

It would be easier of course, to not let them out to play in the snow, but that would also be incredibly mean, knowing how much they enjoy it, so it's a small price to pay, having to spend a few minutes cleaning and thawing them out after a good romp in the white stuff.

10

GROWING OLD GRACEFULLY

I'VE ALWAYS FOUND it strange how some dogs never seem to appear to be growing older, and then suddenly, something happens to make you realise that your dog is no longer a puppy, or indeed, not even young any more. In Penny's case, I think we realised it a couple of years ago. As I've mentioned earlier in the book, most people thought she was an old dog when we first adopted her, because of her white-flecked black facial markings. Even now, at the age of fourteen, she doesn't look much different from the time we first saw her all those years ago at Lisa's home, running around and playing with a deflated football.

It was a couple of years ago, however, that Juliet returned from a walk with Penny and Cassie and told me she thought Penny might have hurt her leg.

"She was limping quite badly on the way home," she reported to me.

"Did she do anything to hurt herself?" I asked.

"No. Cassie was running around like a mad ferret as usual, and Penny was doing her own things, pottering about in the trees and bushes. When I called her to come home, she emerged from the trees, quite happily and came to me to get her lead on. Cassie came bounding up as she always does, and kept jumping up and down as I tried to clip her lead on. Everything was the way it always is with both of them, but when we started walking again, I noticed that Penny was limping. We stopped and I got down on the ground and inspected her paws, in case she had something stuck in her pad, but I couldn't see anything."

I took a look myself and agreed with Juliet. There was nothing visibly wrong with her paw, but I could see she had a definite limp in her left front leg.

"Maybe she's pulled a muscle or something," I suggested. "Let's give it a couple of days and see if it improves. If not, we'd better get her booked in to the vets, so they can check it over."

We did in fact give it a week, as at first, Penny's leg seemed to improve after two days, but by the end of the week, the limp was back again and it was obvious she had a problem, so I made a phone call and booked her in for an appointment the next day.

Rebecca, the vet, gave Penny a thorough examination the following morning. There was no clear reason for Penny's limp, but Rebecca suspected she might have arthritis and suggested an x-ray to confirm her suspicions. Penny was booked in the next day for the x-rays and sure enough, they confirmed what Rebecca had suspected. Penny was given painkillers to help with her problem, and, over a period of time, the limp all but disappeared, and Penny was showing no ill-effects while out and about on her walks with either Juliet or me. The vet recommended that we stop the medication and see how she would get along for a while, and for the next few months, Penny had us believing the arthritis was being held at bay.

The onset of another winter showed we'd been mistaken, as

Penny's limp suddenly returned with a vengeance, while out walking one cold day. This time, I had no further hesitation in making her an appointment to see the vet, and Rebecca immediately booked her in for x-rays, which showed the mild arthritis she'd exhibited previously had progressed and poor old Penny had definite signs of significant bone degeneration around her joints. Strangely, x-rays of her other legs showed no significant signs of the arthritis affecting her other limbs, being restricted to the one front leg. Rebecca assured me that was quite normal, and that it was possible she might not develop the disease in her other legs, though it was highly likely she would do at some time in the future. So far, Penny's been lucky and the disease continues to be restricted to just that one leg. Even now, over the three years since she was first diagnosed, she has good days when the limp is hardly noticeable. If you could see her, as she sets off for her afternoon walk with Cassie, you'd be amazed at the way these two 'old ladies', both fourteen, going on fifteen years of age, literally try to drag Juliet down the garden path to get to the gate. Off they go like a pair of geriatric greyhounds, heading for the big playing field, where, for half an hour or so, the years fall away and they enjoy themselves like a pair of overgrown pups. Penny struts her way along the street with her tail high in the air, her 'flagpole' just missing an ensign to trail in the wind from the tip.

To help her arthritis, Penny, in company with some of our other senior dogs, now takes Glucosamine Sulphate tablets, and Omega 3 capsules in her food on a daily basis, which we've found to be extremely beneficial in helping her joints to stay supple and less painful. When and if she has a period of intense pain, which shows by spells of more aggravated limping, she goes onto a three-day course of Metacam liquid painkiller, which usually brings things under control once more. We've been told by our vet that Omega 3 is also beneficial for a dog's brain too. Now, while that might be true of Sasha, who has them to help with her epilepsy, nothing seems to boost the brain power of little Cassie, whose brain seems to function much the same as always, i.e. She's still is as mad as a ferret, (no change there, then). Seriously though, the Glucosamine/Omega 3 combination has worked well for Penny and the other dogs who are now taking them as they enter their later years.

So, Penny is getting older, but nothing seems to stop her from enjoying life, which is exactly as we would want it. Our little 'railway pup' has grown up in a house filled with love for her and our other dogs, and as she heads towards her fifteenth year, she just goes on enjoying her life, though her days of playing with balls, her frisbee, and even her sticks, are now behind her. That doesn't mean she can't have fun, as she loves nothing more than exploring the small copses that surround the big playing field, playing under the trees and bushes, until she suddenly emerges and starts running around in large circles on the grass, her flagpole tail standing straight up as her little short legs carry her at top speed until she finally decides to return to Juliet. Cassie, meanwhile does her own thing, either performing her own investigations of the bushes or joining in with the games of the other dogs who usually join Juliet at the afternoon 'dog club' get-together. She's still quite likely to steal another dog's ball, and woe-betide whoever tries to get it back from her. She's still so fast that she can outrun any human who attempts to relieve her of her ill-gotten gains. Very often, she's returned home with some other poor dog's ball held firmly between her teeth, only giving it up when she's 'cornered' by Juliet in the utility room, before she and Penny are once again returned to their privileged place in the lounge, to wait for their next highlight of the day, feeding time!

Penny, by comparison with Cassie and our other dogs, is a

real 'lady'. She's quiet and sedate, only barking if she hears someone knocking on the door, and we soon put a stop to that. With eleven dogs in the house, you might be forgiven for thinking they all bark when there's a knock on the door, but in fact, only Penny and three others indulge in 'guard' duty. It's as if, between them, the dogs have all assumed various 'jobs' within the pack, and Penny, Sheba, Dylan and Honey have the 'early warning' responsibility. Sasha is the definite 'pack leader,' who somehow seems to maintain an almost eerie psychological control over the others. None of them will ever do anything to upset Sasha. Muffin and Honey also seem to have the shared responsibility of being the 'jokers in the pack.' If there's mischief afoot, you can bet that either or both of these little scamps will be behind it.

Ah, I may hear some of my regular readers say, "Who's Honey?"

'Mummy' Sasha & Honey

Well, just over a year ago, in November to be precise, my step-daughter, Victoria arrived home one early evening, and as she walked in to the house, she said to Juliet, "Mum, I need you to come outside for a minute."

"What for? What's wrong?" Juliet answered, wondering if Victoria was in some kind of trouble.

"Nothing's wrong. I just need you to come outside for a minute."

Juliet duly followed her through the door and returned a couple of minutes later, holding a very tiny, tan coloured puppy in her arms.

"What's that?" I asked, hardly daring to anticipate the reply. Victoria had been asking if we could have a new puppy for months, and we'd both told her we didn't want any more dogs. Juliet and I aren't getting any younger. We'd already decided a year earlier that we wouldn't add any more dogs to our pack and that if and when we lost any of our current pack, we wouldn't be replacing them.

"Victoria says it's my Christmas present," Juliet replied.

"What? After all the times we've told her we don't want any more dogs?"

"I know, but she just went to a car outside, the door opened and the woman in the car handed the puppy to her, passed her it's bed and a couple of toys, said goodbye, and drove off. So it looks like we're stuck with it."

We were both angry that Victoria had ignored everything we'd said about not having any more dogs, but of course, who can resist the allure of an eight-week old puppy, with its little wagging tail and cheeky face. Victoria walked in, carrying the little dog's bed, blanket, and toys and I gave her a half-hearted telling off; There was little point in being mad at her, as for better or worse, I knew we had little choice in the matter. She assured me and her mum that she would pay for the puppy's inoculations and insurance from her wages, and would walk it regularly once it was allowed out in public after it was fully covered by its injections. Sounded great eh? Over a year later, I'm still waiting for the money for her insurance and inoculations, (no chance of ever getting that back, I think), and within weeks of the puppy's arrival, Victoria left her job and moved to live and work in Scarborough, so Juliet and I were left to fit the puppy, whom Victoria had named Honey, into our daily walking routine. Within days, of course, we were madly in love with our new arrival and Honey was instantly accepted by all the dogs in the pack. They clearly knew she was nothing more than a baby and treated her accordingly. Penny took to her at once, and fussed over her and gave her lots of little 'doggie kisses' in those first few days, and really made Honey feel welcome. Maybe it was the fact that Penny was growing older, because this was the first time we'd seen her behave like this towards a puppy. She'd definitely not displayed such behaviour towards Digby, Muffin and Petal on their arrival into the family.

Of course, our natural 'surrogate mother', Sasha, assumed the major responsibility for looking after the new arrival. As she'd shown with the three pups, (who we still refer to as 'the puppies') even though they're six years old now, she now did exactly the same with little Honey, looking after her as though she was her natural mother. Even though Honey is now well over a year old, the two of them still spend hours playing together, and it's always Sasha who calls the shots and decides when playtime is over. Watching them together is sheer joy, as they run and chase each other, play-fighting and rolling around together. To see them in action, nobody would guess how ill Sasha is, with her epilepsy and skin allergies. Penny and the other dogs just watch them as if they're both mad, though now and then, Sheba and Muffin will join in their high jinks, though they soon drop out and leave Sasha and Honey to carry on their games.

Penny, Petal and Sasha pause for a biscuit break

As she's grown older, Penny has now begun to slow down a lot, although, as evidenced by her attempts to pull Juliet through the garden gate for her afternoon walk, her mind hasn't yet communicated that fact to her body. Once they reach the playing field however, Juliet has seen a marked difference in Penny's activity levels. She's now content to just 'potter' around under the bushes and takes a lot longer to trot across the field when Juliet calls her to go home. She'll even stop now and then for a little rest. Cassie, meanwhile, shows no sign of slowing down, and when seen together, it becomes more obvious that Penny really is ageing much faster than her little companion.

Sometimes, it's hard to believe that Penny has been with us for over twelve years now. Yet, in that time, she's had such fun, and has seen six of our other dogs leave our lives, with numerous new arrivals joining our rescue pack, as she's continued to enjoy her life as part of our family. It's hard to believe that she was once that little pup, abandoned and tied to a railway track, and only rescued by those two brave little girls who took a risk by straying on to the tracks to save her from what would probably have been certain death from the next train that happened along. Thankfully, that particular stretch of the railway isn't one of the busier main line tracks, so not so many trains use it through each day.

So, we can only hope that our little 'railway pup' will be with us for some time to come. Penny's a happy and contented girl, just what we try to achieve with all our rescue dogs. She will be fifteen this year, and we look forward to celebrating her birthday, (which we've estimated based on when she was found), and many more. We hope she'll have a 'pawsome day' and go on to enjoy a few more as part of our rescue pack.

Penny on completion of the book, all fluffed up.

So for now, from me and from Penny, and all our dogs, it's not so much goodbye, more a case of, "See you in the next book."

Love from all of us xxxx

ACKNOWLEDGMENTS

I owe thanks to quite a few people who have been instrumental in enabling me to complete this fourth book in my series, detailing the lives of our pack of rescue dogs.

First and foremost is my dear wife, Juliet, who does most of the work when it comes to caring for our little rescue pack. As a qualified groomer, she's the one who keeps the dogs looking in tip-top condition, spending hours of her time each week, grooming and when necessary, trimming the longer-haired dogs to keep them looking good, as well ensuring their coats are shorter in the summer to help them stay cool, and then of course, keeping them neat and tidy as we let their fur grows longer in the winter. She's also the chief critic of my work, and soon lets me know if I'm rambling on too much, correcting any errors of memory that may creep into the narrative, (I'm not getting any younger either these days), thus keeping the facts of the story on the right track. (Right track, railway pup, get it?).

As with all my books, I owe a huge debt of thanks to my good friend, proof reader and researcher, Debbie Poole. Living in Liverpool, Debbie, together with her research assistant, Dot

Blackman, has been instrumental in ensuring a degree of accuracy in my Mersey Mystery series that I would seriously fail in if left to my own devices. It's been many years since I was 'at home' in the city and Liverpool's geography, topography, even individual streets and buildings have changed so much that it is definitely not the city I knew as a child. Together, these two intrepid ladies have driven many miles around the Merseyside area, checking out addresses, appropriate murder sites and locations suitable for 'body dumps' etc. and have, I'm sure, drawn a few worried glances from passers-by and perhaps the odd police officer as they hang over bridge parapets, examine areas of little used undergrowth and so on.

While Debbie's work as a researcher isn't necessary for my dog rescue books, her services as a proof reader and her critique of each chapter has proved invaluable, helping me to avoid errors and repetition, something I'm prone to do when talking about my four legged friends.

Thanks also to Rebecca Aldren and the other vets, nurses and staff at the Wheatley, Doncaster, branch of Vets 4 Pets, the veterinary practice that has taken care of Penny and all our dogs for over the last twelve years. Without their help and professional care, many of our dogs wouldn't be with us today.

Of course, thanks must go to my publisher, Miika Hannila and the staff at Creativia Publishing for their ongoing support, promotion and marketing of my books. They do a fantastic job, for which I'll always be grateful.

Finally, I owe massive thanks to my readers, especially those who have faithfully followed my work for years. My mystery/thrillers, dog rescue books and my occasional poetry collections have all been successful to varying degrees, all of which is attributable to my growing army of regular readers.

Thank you all, from the bottom of my heart.

ABOUT THE AUTHOR

Brian L Porter is an award-winning, bestselling author, whose books have regularly topped the Amazon Best Selling charts. Writing as Brian, he has won a Best Author Award and his mystery/thrillers have picked up Best Thriller and Best Mystery Awards. The third book in his Mersey Mystery series, *A Mersey Maiden* recently won The Best Book We've Read all Year Award, 2018, from Readfree,ly. In addition, *Cassie's Tale* was the runner-up in the 2018 Top 50 Best Indie Boks of the year, at the same time winning the Non-fiction category, and *A Very Mersey Murder* finished in 5th place in the same awards, while also winning the Best Mystery Novel Award.

When it comes to dogs and dog rescue, he is passionate about the subject and his three previous dog rescue books have been hugely successful. Sasha: A Very Special Dog Tale of a Very Special Epi-Dog is now an award-winning international bestseller and Sheba: From Hell to Happiness is also a UK Bestseller and an award winner too. *Cassie's Tale*, the third book in the series, also followed Sasha and Sheba in winning the Critters.org, (formerly Preditors and Editors), annual Best Non-fiction award, 2018, and there are sure to be more to follow.

Writing as Harry Porter his children's books have achieved three bestselling rankings on Amazon in the USA and UK.

In addition, his third incarnation as romantic poet Juan Pablo Jalisco has brought international recognition with his collected works, *Of Aztecs and Conquistadors* topping the best-selling charts in the USA, UK and Canada.

Brian lives with his wife,one step-daughter and of course, Sasha and the rest of his wonderful pack of ten rescued dogs, in the North of England.

A Mersey Killing and the subsequent books in his Mersey Mystery series have already been optioned for adaptation as a TV series, in addition to his other novels, all of which have been signed by ThunderBall Films in a movie franchise deal.

See Brian's website at http://www.brianlporter.co.uk

You can find the Rescuedog series, (Family of Rescuedogs) at http://viewbook.at/rescuedogs

Sasha has her own Facebook page, which contains information about all the dogs, at Sasha the Wagging Tail of England https://www.facebook.com/groups/270003923193039/

And all the Mersey Mystery series is at http://getbook.at/MerseyMysteries

Brian's blog is at https://sashaandharry.blogspot.com/

You can find all his books by visiting his author page at Amazon

The award-winning Rescuedog series

OTHER BOOKS BY BRIAN PORTER

Dog Rescue Series

Sasha – A Very Special Dog Tale of a Very Special Epi-Dog

Sheba: From Hell to Happiness

Cassie's Tale

Thrillers by Brian L Porter

A Study in Red - The Secret Journal of Jack the Ripper

Legacy of the Ripper

Requiem for the Ripper

Pestilence

Purple Death

Behind Closed Doors

Avenue of the Dead

The Nemesis Cell

Kiss of Life

The Mersey Mystery Series

A Mersey Killing (Amazon bestseller)

All Saints, Murder on the Mersey

A Mersey Maiden

A Mersey Mariner

A Very Mersey Murder

Last Train to Lime Street

(Coming soon) – The Mersey Monastery Murders

Short Story Collections

After Armageddon (Amazon bestseller)

Remembrance Poetry

Lest We Forget (Amazon bestseller)

Children's books as Harry Porter

Wolf (Amazon bestseller)

Alistair the Alligator, (Illustrated by Sharon Lewis) (Amazon bestseller)

Charlie the Caterpillar (Illustrated by Bonnie Pelton) (Amazon bestseller)

As Juan Pablo Jalisco

Of Aztecs and; Conquistadors (Amazon bestseller)

Bye bye

Author's footnote: Just prior to the book going to the layout stage,
Creativa decided to do a revamp of the covers of all the Family of
Recuedogs series, and the new-look covers are shown here. It's
interesting to note that while on pre-order, Penny the Railway Pup
became the #1 Best Selling new release on Amazon.com and was also
a bestseller in Australia and Canada.

Made in United States
Orlando, FL
02 August 2023